A

METHOD

OF

TEACHING HARMONY

BASED UPON

SYSTEMATIC EAR-TRAINING

AND UPON THE

HARMONIZATION OF UNFIGURED BASSES, FIGURED
BASSES AND MELODIES, AND THE CONSTRUCTION
OF HARMONIC PROGRESSIONS BY THE PUPIL.

BY

FREDERICK G. SHINN,

MUS. DOC., DUNELM, A.R.C.M., F.R.C.O.

PROFESSOR OF THE ART OF TEACHING, OF EAR-TRAINING AND MUSICAL DICTATION, AND OF
HARMONY AT THE GUILDHALL SCHOOL OF MUSIC.

PART I.—DIATONIC HARMONY.

Price 2s. 6d.   Cloth boards, 3/6 net.

LONDON:
THE VINCENT MUSIC COMPANY LIMITED,
60, BERNERS STREET, W.

MUSICAL EDUCATIONAL WORKS

BY

FREDERICK G. SHINN.

ELEMENTARY EAR-TRAINING.

Book I.—MELODIC.

Second (enlarged) Edition, with Appendix of 100 Melodies (original and selected), which include 60 illustrations of old Dance Tunes, taken from the Fitzwilliam Virginal Book and other sources.

Price Two Shillings.

Book II.—HARMONIC AND CONTRAPUNTAL.

PART I. HARMONIC EAR-TRAINING.—A method of ear-training in connection with intervals, chords and progressions of such, supplemented with a large number of harmonic dictation exercises carefully graduated in length and difficulty.

PART II. CONTRAPUNTAL EAR-TRAINING –A method of ear-training in connection with musical progressions of a contrapuntal character, supplemented with a large number of dictation exercises in two, three and four parts, carefully graduated in length and difficulty, and partly selected from the works of the greatest composers, from Palestrina to Schumann. Many of the original exercises in three and four parts have been written with the object of training the listener to specially direct his attention towards the inner part or parts.

Price Three Shillings.

A METHOD OF TEACHING HARMONY,

BASED UPON

SYSTEMATIC EAR-TRAINING,

and upon the Harmonization of Unfigured Basses, Figured Basses and Melodies, and the Construction of Harmonic Progressions by the Pupil.

PART I DIATONIC HARMONY (including the chord of the Dominant Seventh, Passing Notes, Suspensions and Simple Modulation).

PART II. CHROMATIC HARMONY AND EXCEPTIONAL PROGRESSION (with a chapter upon the Harmonization of Ground Basses).

Price of each Part, Two Shillings and Sixpence. In cloth boards, Three Shillings.

MUSICAL MEMORY AND ITS CULTIVATION.

PART I - An investigation into the forms of memory employed in Pianoforte Playing, and a theory as to the relative extent of the employment of such forms

PART II.—The Cultivation of Musical Memory—a Guide to the Memorization of Piano Music.

Price Two Shillings and Sixpence,

Press opinions upon the above works will be found at the end of this book

AUTHOR'S NOTE.

THE addition of another text book to the many already published text books upon Harmony, seems to call for some explanation The author believes that an adequate explanation, as well as some justification for the publication of the present work, may be found in the plan of the book itself, and that the method of teaching Harmony herein expounded differs very considerably from any already published method, at least, so far as the author's knowledge of such methods extends Moreover, he believes, that many teachers, whose number is increasing every day, will find set forth herein, a complete and systematic method of teaching Harmony, based upon similar fundamental principles to those upon which their own teaching has been based, although, possibly developed in a more complete and comprehensive manner than that which they have been able to employ, owing to the absence of any book containing suitable graduated exercises. It is hoped that the present work will supply this very obvious deficiency amongst musical educational works, which no teacher has felt more keenly than the author himself.

The author wishes to gratefully acknowledge the many valuable suggestions which he has received from his friends, Dr. H. A. Harding, Mr. Orlando Morgan, Dr. H. W. Richards, and also to Dr. Hamilton Robinson who has kindly corrected some of the proof sheets.

SYDENHAM, *May 1904.*

TABLE OF CONTENTS.

[The numbers always refer to the Paragraphs, *except in those instances in which it is otherwise stated.]*

PART I.

DIATONIC HARMONY.

TO THE TEACHER.

I T may possibly help those who make use of this book, if their
attention is drawn, in a preliminary chapter, to the chief points in
which this text book differs from other text books upon the same
subject, and, it may also help them to understand the author's point of
view, when he leaves the beaten track, if, to an enumeration of these
differences, is added a brief summary of the reasons which caused them
to be made, and which he believes fully justifies them.

The most characteristic feature of this method, and the feature which,
the author believes, distinguishes it from all other published methods, is,
that it is based upon *direct harmonic ear-training*. In other words, the
end, which, first of all, it is specially designed to accomplish, is the
training of the pupil's ear to discriminate and to recognize each chord
by its sound, and then, the training of his musical memory to retain the
sound of each individual chord, and to associate such sound with the
correct notational signs   For these purposes Ear Exercises are supplied
in connection with every chord, and they are the *first* exercises or tests,
to which the pupil is subjected to in connection with any chord. These
exercises are to be played by the teacher upon the piano, or other
keyboard instrument, and then written down by the pupil from their
sound.

Although, the fact that this method is based upon direct ear-training,
is apparently only one amongst several points of difference, which
distinguishes it from other methods, yet, the other differences which
exist are very largely due to this.   One of the most important of
these differences is the individual attention which is given to each
chord, and to each inversion of a chord   Especially will this be
noticeable in connection with the diatonic triads and their inversions,
where, with the exception of a few second inversions, each is treated
separately. It must be obvious that to each combination of notes
(whether such is an original position of a chord or an inversion) belongs
a particular musical effect, and also, each has its own special function
and position amongst the chords of a key, and if these characteristic

properties of each chord are to be thoroughly understood, the various chords must in the first instance be so introduced, that the attention can be concentrated upon the distinguishing features of each individual chord. In order to achieve this end, *the chords, and their different inversions, must be presented to the pupil* ONE AT A TIME Starting with a single chord, the teacher must proceed chord by chord, and inversion by inversion, until he has completed the whole harmonic fabric. Upon no other method is it possible to teach Harmony, based on ear-training, in a thoroughly complete, systematic and satisfactory manner.

Two of the chief objectives which this method has in view, then, are, (1) the imparting of a knowledge of chords based primarily upon their sound, and (2) a study of their nature and function, first, individually, and then, joined with others to form progressions If, however, we claim to teach these aspects of the various chords, it is necessary that the exercises given upon each chord should test the pupil's knowledge, and exercise his powers in these special directions.   That is, the working of the Exercises, given in connection with the various chords, must reveal, at least to some extent, how far the pupil can hear, mentally, the sound of the chords he has written down, and, by his ability to frame satisfactory progressions of them, how far he under-stands their individual nature and function Hitherto, in most Harmony text books, the Exercises employed have been principally, if not entirely, in the form of Figured basses, but it only requires a brief consideration of the nature of such exercises, and of the directions in which they furnish *no test* whatever, to show, that, for the above mentioned purposes, exercises of this kind are quite useless. First of all, the filling up of Figured basses cannot test the pupil's power of hearing. mentally, what he is writing down, for it is quite possible to correctly fill up the parts of an exercise in accordance with the figures, without having any idea of the musical effect of the resulting harmonic progressions Secondly, the filling up of Figured basses neither exercises nor tests in the slightest degree the pupil's knowledge of the function of the individual chords, nor his power of selecting chords, which shall be suitable to join with others, for the formation of satisfactory harmonic progressions, for all such matters are decided for him.   In these two most essential matters, exercises in the form of Figured basses supply *no test* whatever, and, therefore, although the Figured bass has hitherto been the time-honoured servant, or hack, of every harmony teacher, yet in this book such exercises have been relegated to a position, more, we think, in accordance with the small intrinsic value which they possess as instruments for the teaching of Harmony, than they have hitherto held

If, then, the Figured Bass exercise be inadequate for the efficient teaching of Harmony, the question arises, what kind of exercise should take its place? We believe that the matters which we insist should be tested by Harmony exercises, can only be adequately tested, as far as written exercises are concerned, by those exercises which leave the selection of the chords almost entirely to the pupil Apart from the writing of absolutely original progressions, the only exercises which admit of this freedom of harmonization are Unfigured basses and Melodies, and these are the two forms of exercises which we have almost entirely adopted in this method In connection with the various discords, in addition however, to such exercises, the pupil is required to construct short progressions, similar in form to the Ear Exercises, which shall illustrate the different resolutions of the special chord under consideration, while in order that the pupil may understand the method of indicating chords by means of figures, which, as a method of "musical shorthand" has distinct value, a small number of Figured Basses are included, after the other exercises given in connection with the various chords.

Before leaving the subject of Harmony exercises, it may not be inappropriate, to suggest some explanation as to the causes which led to the almost universal adoption of the Figured Bass as an instrument for the teaching of Harmony. There can be little doubt that this was originally due to the custom which prevailed up to the early part of the nineteenth century, of indicating instrumental accompaniments by means of figured basses. As a general rule, the harpsichord (or organ) accompaniments to operas and oratorios were written either simply as a figured bass, or else as a figured bass with the highest part in addition This made it necessary for accompanists to understand how to correctly supply either the whole of the upper parts, or, at least, the inner parts, from the figures, and the ability to play with readiness and accuracy from a figured (or what was frequently called a Thorough) bass became the indispensable possession of every musician It was doubtless in order to acquire this power that many musical students, in the first instance, entered upon the study of Harmony, and it is therefore not difficult to understand, how a knowledge of chords, as represented by figures under a bass part, and the ability to correctly fill up such a bass, either upon paper, or at the keyboard, gradually came to be regarded as synonymous with a knowledge of Harmony. During the last century, however, the methods of composers underwent a very considerable change in the manner of recording their compositions, and the custom of leaving the details of their works to be filled in by the executant, from a figured bass, is now never resorted to, whilst even in works in which this was formerly done, the modern editor has stepped in and supplied the deficiency. At the present time, therefore, it is only upon those exceptional occasions, when an *old edition of an old work*, is made use of, that the performer is now called upon to do, what a hundred years ago was a matter of daily occurrence. This change in the methods of composers, depreciated, to a very considerable extent, the value of the figured bass exercise as an instrument for the teaching of Harmony While one of the chief objects of the study of Harmony was to acquire the power of interpreting figured basses, it was necessary that the filling up of figured basses should enter, very largely, into the study of Harmony, when, however, facility in interpreting the figures, no longer remains the prime object, or even an important object in the study of Harmony, figured bass exercises must be judged according to the intrinsic merit they possess as instruments for the teaching of Harmony, and this we believe to be very small. It is a curious fact that teachers and writers upon Harmony, have, for years, failed to perceive this, and hitherto have made few attempts to systematically supplement figured basses with other and more valuable forms of exercises. With a conservatism, worthy of a better cause, they have held on to the beaten track, and finally, have exalted the figured bass exercise to such a unique position in the teaching of Harmony, and in Harmony examinations, that the present-day student is still encouraged to cherish the belief, that, upon the successful working of an unlimited number of figured basses rests his one and only hope of harmonic salvation.

To one other point only, in connection with this method, generally, is it necessary to direct the attention of the teacher, that is, to the *order* which has been adopted, in the arrangement of the materials of the subject, not merely with regard to the chords themselves, but also with regard to the rules which govern their formation and progression. With reference to the CHORDS, an order which is suitable for teaching purposes must be satisfactory from two points of view: (1), it must show the chords in the order in which the mind can most readily receive and assimilate them as combinations of musical sounds, and (2), it must also show them in an order which will give to the student clear ideas as to their systematic formation and classification. The *first condition* requires, that the chords, with the sound of which the pupil is familiar (owing to the influence of his general musical environment) should be introduced before those, with the sound of which he is less familiar, and these later ones before those which are comparatively unknown to him. The *second condition* requires, that the order employed shall exemplify the regular and gradual building up of the various chords upon some intelligible plan. To frame an order in which the requirements of both of these conditions should be completely satisfied is practically impossible; it is therefore necessary, that, in every method of teaching Harmony, the order in which the chords are presented, must represent a compromise between these two conditions, and the nature of this compromise, that is, the exact order adopted, must be decided by the author of the method. Whether those using this book feel that the order given herein is satisfactory, or prefer to modify it in some of its details, is unimportant; what is important, is, that they should understand the underlying principles upon which this or any other suitable order for teaching purposes, must be framed

With regard to the RULES which regulate the progression of the several chords, or the progression of one or more notes of a chord, generally called the " Rules of Melodic and Harmonic Progression," such are not introduced until the pupil is ready to make immediate use of them ; for instance, the pupil is not informed that "consecutive perfect fourths with the bass are forbidden" until he is able to use two $\frac{6}{4}$ chords upon consecutive bass notes, neither is he told that "consecutive seconds and sevenths between any two parts are forbidden" until he is familiar with chords which admit of such progressions   As he approaches new tracts of country where he will require fresh directions, new sign posts are supplied, but they are not supplied till they are required.

Having reviewed the general principles which underlie the method employed in this book, we will now refer quite briefly to a few points of detail.   One of the most important of these, is the equal attention which must be given to the various chords in both Major and Minor keys, in all the different forms of Exercises.   The limitations of space have compelled us to omit all but a few Ear Exercises in the Minor key, for by employing almost entirely the Major key in such exercises, we have been enabled to give a far more complete and varied series of Ear Exercises than would have been possible, had we made equal use of both keys.   It therefore devolves upon the teacher to transpose the large majority of such exercises from the Major key into the Tonic Minor key, and *this must invariably be done, whenever separate Ear Exercises in the Minor key are not given* *   The operation of transposition, which thus becomes necessary, is not however, otherwise, an entirely useless one, for it directs the attention of both teacher and pupil to a most important fact in connection with chords generally, and which is sometimes overlooked or partly so, namely, that after due allowance has been made for the characteristic differences between the Major scale and the Minor scale, the function and progression of most chords, does not essentially differ in major and minor keys having the same key-note.

* This transposition from the key of C major to that of C minor should present no difficulty, it being merely a mental prefixing of the key signature of C minor with three flats, while keeping the B's natural.

There are of course some exercises which, if transposed from the Major key to the Tonic Minor key, owing to the differences in the nature of the two scales, incorrect melodic or harmonic progressions would be created. Where such incorrect progressions would arise, the exercises are not marked for transposition In addition to the Ear Exercises given, others illustrating the various chords, but showing them in different keys and with the several notes differently distributed, should be supplied by the teacher (see note, page 16 *₊*).

Besides those exercises which are specially described as Ear Exercises, *the teacher should make it a regular practice to employ as an Ear Exercise* (that is, as an exercise to be written down by the pupil from dictation) *every musical example which illustrates a correct progression,* and he should also employ as an Ear Exercise, although *not* to be written down, but carefully listened to, every musical example which illustrates an incorrect progression. Thus the ear should be trained to discriminate by their sound between progressions which are regarded as correct, and those which are regarded as incorrect.

The manner of dictating the Ear Exercises, and the number of times it will be necessary to play them over to a pupil in order that he may be able to write them down, must of course depend upon the natural aural capacity of the pupil, both with regard to the discriminative power or fineness of his ear, and also his retentive power for musical sounds generally. The average pupil, in the early stages, will probably require several repetitions for even quite short exercises, and it may be a considerable time before he will be able to remember progressions of more than two or three different chords played consecutively, that is to say, exercises of four or more different chords, will have to be dictated in a piece-meal manner. All such matters however can only be decided by the teacher for each individual pupil.

With regard to the written exercises, which involve the harmonization of a Bass or Melody by the pupil, (and which should also be supple- mented by others supplied by the teacher whenever additional ones are required), the note at the top of page 38 *₊*, referring to the systematic analysis and figuring of the chords employed in such, should be carefully attended to, and consistently enforced in connection with every exercise worked by the pupil. The requirements of all the written exercises have been designed so as to make the pupil responsible for as much as possible in the working of them, and yet, not more than he should be able to successfully accomplish, if he has studied thoroughly, and really mastered what has preceded any set of exercises. THE VALUE AND IMPORTANCE OF A PUPIL DOING THINGS HIMSELF, RATHER THAN MERELY READING ABOUT THEM AND LOOKING AT EXAMPLES WRITTEN BY OTHERS, CANNOT BE OVERESTIMATED The author does not hesitate to state, that, the working of the numerous construction exercises upon the model of the Ear Exercises, given in connection with the chord of the Dominant Seventh, Modulation, Unessential Notes, and Suspensions, in which everything is left for the pupil to do, will teach him more about these various matters and the way of overcoming their characteristic difficulties, than reading many text books and filling up hundreds of figured basses.

A METHOD OF TEACHING HARMONY.

PART I.

DIATONIC HARMONY.

CHAPTER I.

HARMONY AND ITS SUBJECT MATTER.

1. HARMONY treats of the nature, classification and treatment of chords or musical sounds heard in combination. It does not deal with chords merely in their notational representation, as seems sometimes to be imagined, but is concerned with them, *primarily, as musical effects* Chords exist quite apart from any form of musical notation by which they may be represented, just as the objects which surround us exist, quite apart from the name by which they are known, and the manner of writing that name in any language. As in everyday life we require words by which to refer to different things, supplemented by the art of writing by which we may record facts about them, so, in dealing with chords, either in connection with Musical Composition, or in the more elementary studies (such as Harmony and Counterpoint) which lead up to this, it is necessary that there should be some generally understood method of bringing them before the mind, through the medium of the eye (that is, by writing), and also of recording them with some degree of permanence. This is done by the employment of Musical Notation, and of the signs belonging thereto With this notation and its signs however, Harmony is only *indirectly* concerned It is the sounds which lie behind, and are represented by the signs, and which the sight of the signs should instantly recall to the mind, that the study of Harmony is *directly* concerned *These sounds, heard in combination, are the essential things*, with the nature, classification, and treatment of which, Harmony specially concerns itself. To the student of Harmony, there is no fact of greater importance than this, and upon its due recognition, success or failure in the mastery of the subject almost entirely depends

2. It is obvious, therefore, that *as the study of each chord is entered upon, its musical character must first of all be considered* The rules referring to the special treatment a chord may require, will doubtless furnish knowledge of a most valuable kind as to its correct grammatical employment, but it is knowledge which should *follow*, and not precede, knowledge of the sound of the chord itself. It matters not how familiar the student becomes with the rules of Harmony, the power he will acquire of effectively employing the various chords, in the formation of

harmonic progressions (and this is the ultimate aim of the study of Harmony), will almost entirely depend upon the extent to which he can memorize their sound, and mentally recall this at the sight of their respective notational signs. Before a chord is employed in written exercises, its effect in sound, therefore should, to some extent, have been memorized by the ear. Only when this has been done will it be possible to create in the mind any clear idea of the sound of the progressions which are being written down, and unless this can be done, and *is done, systematically, in connection with all written exercises*, the study of Harmony loses its living musical character and becomes merely a study of lifeless and meaningless signs.

3. In these few remarks we have endeavoured to lead the student towards the adoption of a correct attitude of mind with regard to the study of Harmony and the nature of chords in general; * before proceeding to a detailed consideration of the different chords, there are, however, two matters which claim our consideration. The *first* of these refers to the relationship existing between the individual notes which together make up what is called a *Key*, and which furnish the material from which chords are constructed. These and other related matters are treated of in the following chapter. The *second* refers to the manner of measuring and of naming the Intervals formed between the various notes of a key, and to such matters as the Classification and the Inversion of Intervals. Chapter III is devoted to a consideration of these.

* This aspect of the study of Harmony is further discussed in the author's " *Musical Memory and its Cultivation*," in chapters VIII and XII of which, it is considered with more completeness than is possible here.

CHAPTER II.

KEY —THE DIATONIC SCALES

4 A KEY in music is represented by certain musical sounds, which, both with regard to their pitch and also to the manner of writing them, have a definite relation to some one sound or note. This sound or note is described as the KEY-NOTE, and from it the key takes its alphabetical name. To each key-note, however, there belongs two keys, a Major key and a Minor key, both of which take their alphabetical name from this same note, and the key of a passage is described as Major or as Minor according to the prominence given to certain notes of the key.

5 The several notes which together make up a key are twelve in number. They are situated at the distance of a semitone from each other, and are all included within the interval of an octave. Any of them, however, may be duplicated by being sounded one, or more, octaves higher or lower, as the compass of musical instruments may permit. When the notes of a key are heard as a regular succession of sounds, either ascending or descending, they form what is called a SCALE A Scale in which all the twelve notes are employed is called a *Chromatic Scale*, thus :—

Ex. 1.

Key-note

The notation of this Scale is explained in Chap. XXIV (Part II).

Scales in which only an alphabetical succession of the notes of the key are employed, are called *Diatonic Scales*.

6 **The Diatonic Scales.**—The Diatonic Scales comprise the *Major Scale*, and the two forms of the *Minor Scale*, the Harmonic form and the Melodic or Arbitrary form The MAJOR SCALE has semitones between the third and fourth degrees, and the seventh and eighth degrees, and tones between all the other adjacent degrees, thus :—

Ex 2.

1   2   3   4   5   6   7   8

The HARMONIC MINOR SCALE is so called because it forms the basis of harmonic combinations in the minor key. It may be formed by lowering

B

the third and sixth degrees of the major scale a semitone. This form of
the minor scale will be found to have semitones between the second and
third, fifth and sixth, and seventh and eighth degrees, an augmented
second (three semitones) between the sixth and seventh degrees, and
tones between all the other adjacent degrees.

The MELODIC OR ARBITRARY MINOR SCALE is so called because by an
arbitrary alteration of the previous scale, in the employment of the
major sixth and major seventh ascending, and the minor seventh and
minor sixth descending, the interval of the augmented second is
avoided, and the scale is thus made more suitable for employment for
melodic purposes. In this form of the minor scale semitones occur
between the second and third, and seventh and eighth degrees ascending,
and between the fifth and sixth and second and third degrees descending,
and tones between all the other adjacent degrees.

7. **Major Scales and their Key-Signatures.**—In the
construction of the Major scales, every scale, with the exception of the
scale of C major, requires the employment of one or more sharps or flats,
in order that the tones and semitones may occur in their proper relative
order. With regard to the scales requiring sharps, the scale which requires the employment of one sharp for its correct formation begins on
the fifth note of the scale of C, that is G, and the note which requires to
be sharpened is F the seventh note from G. The scale which requires
the employment of two sharps begins on D, the fifth note of the
scale of G, and the notes which require to be sharpened are F and C.
The scale which requires three sharps begins on A the fifth note
of the scale of D and the notes which require to be sharpened are
F, C, and G, and so on until the scale of F sharp with six sharps is
reached. With regard to the scales requiring flats, the scale which requires
the employment of one flat begins on the fifth note of the scale of C
counting downwards, that is F, and the note which requires to be flattened is B, the fifth note from F *counting downwards*. The scale which
involves the employment of two flats begins on B flat, the fifth note
from F counting *down* the scale of F, and the note which requires to be
flattened, in addition to B, is E. The scale which has three flats begins
on E flat, the fifth note counting down the scale of B flat, and so on
until the scale of G flat with six flats is reached. A comparison of this
scale (G flat with six flats) with the scale of F sharp with six sharps, will
show that the only difference between these two scales is one of notation;
when played upon keyboard instruments they are absolutely identical.

The employment of keys requiring more than six sharps or six flats in the signature is rare, as such keys would have equivalent keys possessing a simpler signature. Thus the key of C sharp with seven sharps would correspond to that of D flat with five flats, see Ex. 5 (*b*); and the key of C flat with seven flats, to that of B with five sharps, see Ex. 5 (*a*).

MAJOR KEY SIGNATURES.

Ex. 5.   SHARP KEYS (*a fifth apart counting upwards.*)

(F♯ or G♭)

FLAT KEYS (*a fifth apart counting downwards.*)

8. Minor Scales and their Key-Signatures.—The Minor scales are always written with the key-signature of the Major scale of their third note. The scale of C minor (in either form) is therefore written with the key-signature of E flat major, and has three flats in the signature, as shown in Exs. 6 and 7. This custom of using the same key-signature for both major and minor scales involves the employment of an accidental before the seventh note in all minor scales in their Harmonic form, and also the employment of accidentals before both the sixth and the seventh notes in the *ascending* Melodic form. All these inflected notes, however, are *diatonic* notes in the scale or key to which they belong.

Ex. 6.

HARMONIC MINOR SCALE.

Ex. 7.

MELODIC OR ARBITRARY MINOR SCALE.

The relationship between the key-notes of the Minor scales with regard to the employment of sharps or flats in regular progression is similar to that of the key-notes of the Major scales, that is, by ascending or by descending in fifths respectively. The key-signature of a minor scale has either three flats more or three sharps less than the key-signature of the major scale beginning with the same note, or else it has a signature which is equivalent to this alteration. In Ex. 8 it will be seen that the last three keys have each an equivalent key.

MINOR KEY SIGNATURES.

Ex. 8.

(D♯ or E♭?)

9. The Relationship between Major and Minor Keys.

The employment of the same key-signature for two different keys, one of which is major and the other minor, has given rise to the terms *Relative Major* and *Relative Minor*, which are frequently used to describe keys having a common key-signature. Thus the key of E flat major is the Relative Major of the key of C minor, and the key of C minor is the Relative Minor of the key of E flat major. This so-called relationship rests entirely upon identity of key-signature, although it naturally follows from this that many of the notes of one key are also found in the other. Another form of relationship which may exist between Major and Minor keys is produced when such have the same key-note. They are then described as *Tonic Major* and *Tonic Minor* respectively. Thus, the key of C major is the Tonic Major of the key of C minor, and the key of C minor the Tonic Minor of the key of C major.

10. The Names of the Degrees of the Scale.—Besides

the ordinary alphabetical names which belong to the notes of a scale, each degree of a diatonic scale (Major or Minor) has a special name which defines its relative position in the scale, and by which name it is usually referred to in the study of Harmony. These names are given below, and in an order which will help to explain their derivation and meaning. The different degrees are counted from the first note of the scale *upwards*.

FIRST DEGREE.—*Tonic* or *Key-note*.

FIFTH DEGREE.—*Dominant* (so called because the chords formed upon this note "dominate or command" the key).

FOURTH DEGREE.—*Subdominant* (the fifth degree *below* the Tonic ; the under-dominant).

THIRD DEGREE.—*Mediant* (midway between Tonic and Dominant).

SIXTH DEGREE.—*Submediant* (midway between Tonic and Subdominant counting downwards).

SECOND DEGREE.—*Supertonic* (the note *above* the Tonic).

SEVENTH DEGREE.—*Leading-note* (the note which naturally *leads* to the Tonic).

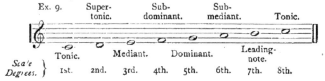

Ex. 9. Super-tonic. Sub-dominant. Sub-mediant. Tonic. Tonic. Mediant. Dominant. Leading-note.

Scale Degrees.} 1st. 2nd. 3rd. 4th. 5th. 6th. 7th. 8th.

EXERCISES.

1 —Write Major Scales beginning with each of the following notes. Place the necessary accidentals before the notes of each Scale as they are required, and the correct key-signature in a separate bar by itself at the end .—

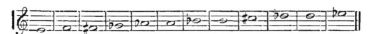

2.—Write, in a similar manner, the Relative Minor Scales (Harmonic Form) of the above Major Scales.

3 —Write the Tonic Minor Scales (Melodic Form) ascending and descending, of the above Major Scales, except G flat and D flat. In this Exercise prefix the correct key-signatures in the usual way.

4 —Name all the scales (Major and Minor) in which each of the following pairs of notes are found · B and F, B and E sharp, F and C flat, F sharp and C, F sharp and B sharp, C and G flat

5 —Name the scales in which each of the following pairs of notes are found . F sharp and E flat, D and E sharp, A and G flat; B and C double sharp, F sharp and G double sharp, D and C flat

6 —Name the scales in which each of the following pairs of notes are found · B sharp and E, D and G flat, A and D flat, E and A flat, D and A sharp, A and E sharp

7 —Name the Dominants and the Leading - notes of the keys of E, F, B and D flat

8 —Name the Supertonics and the Subdominants of the keys of A, B flat, C sharp, and G flat.

9 —Name the Mediants and the Submediants of both the Major and the Minor keys of A flat, F sharp, E flat, and D

CHAPTER III.

INTERVALS—THEIR DEFINITION, CLASSIFICATION, AND INVERSION.

[In this chapter the subject of "Intervals" is discussed only from a theoretical standpoint. The musical·aspect of Intervals, considered with a view to training the ear to discriminate the different intervals by their sound, has already been dealt with by the author in his "*Elementary Ear Training*," the early chapters of which may be regarded as complementary to the present chapter]

11. The difference in pitch between two musical sounds is called an INTERVAL. The exact nature of an Interval is only accurately known when it is defined from two different standpoints, (1) *numerically*, as a second, a third, or a fourth, etc.; and (2) *qualitatively*, as a major interval, a minor interval, or a perfect interval, etc When these two forms of qualification are combined, and such terms as major second, minor third, or perfect fourth, are employed, the difference in pitch between the two notes forming the interval is exactly defined , and, if the name of one of these notes be given, that of the other may be ascertained by a matter of simple calculation

12. "**Numerical**" **Definition.**—Intervals, (which are always reckoned *upwards* unless the contrary be specified), are calculated "numerically" according to the number of notes of different alphabetical names included in the interval. In all such calculations both of the notes which form the interval are counted That in Ex. 10 (*a*), both intervals are fourths because there are four different alphabetical names, C, D, E, and F, included in each interval; while in (*b*), both intervals are fifths because each includes five different names, C, D, E, F, and G.

Ex 10

Although upon all keyboard instruments the notes of the second fourth and the second fifth are identical, yet for theoretical purposes it is necessary that intervals should always be defined according to the manner in which they are represented in musical notation. Speaking then, "numerically," C to F sharp is a fourth, and C to G flat a fifth, in spite of the fact that upon some musical instruments the notes represented and the sound produced would be exactly the same in both cases

13. "**Qualitative**" **Definition.**—In determining the "quality" of an interval, the intervals between the Key-note of the Major scale and the several notes of that scale, counted upwards from the Key-note,

furnish the basis of calculation. All the intervals thus formed are either Perfect intervals, or Major intervals, as is shown in Ex. 11 :—

Ex. 11.

PERFECT. – Unison. – – – – – – 4th. – 5th. – – – – – Octave.

MAJOR. – – – – 2nd. – 3rd. – – – – – 6th. – 7th.

When either Perfect intervals or Major intervals are enlarged by the addition of a semitone, they become Augmented intervals, as will be seen by reference to Ex. 12. When Perfect intervals are reduced by the interval of a semitone they become Diminished intervals, but when Major intervals are reduced by the interval of a semitone they become Minor intervals, which Minor intervals being further reduced by a semitone become Diminished. A Diminished fifth is frequently called an "Imperfect" fifth, but the term "Imperfect" is not similarly used as an alternative in connection with either the fourth or the octave. Ex. 12 illustrates the various modifications which intervals undergo :—

Ex. 12.

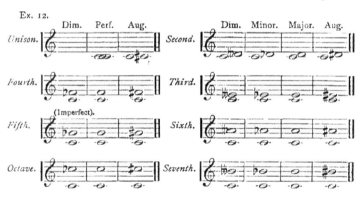

14. **Classification of Intervals.**—Intervals may be classified in three different ways : (1) as *Consonant* or *Dissonant*, (2) as *Diatonic* or *Chromatic*, and (3) as *Simple* or *Compound*.

15. **Consonant and Dissonant Intervals.**—A *Consonant interval* is an interval which produces a more or less complete and satisfactory musical effect when heard by itself, as the Perfect fifth (*a*) shown below ; while a *Dissonant interval* is one which produces an incomplete musical effect when heard by itself, as the Minor seventh shown at (*b*).

The CONSONANT INTERVALS comprise all the Perfect intervals (perfect fourth, perfect fifth and perfect octave) and the major and minor thirds and sixths. The Perfect intervals are called *Perfect consonances* because they cannot be altered in any direction (that is by augmentation or diminution) without becoming dissonant. The thirds and sixths are called *Imperfect consonances* because they have two forms, major and minor, in both of which they are consonant. The DISSONANT INTERVALS comprise the major and minor seconds and sevenths and all Augmented and Diminished intervals.

16. **Diatonic and Chromatic Intervals.**—All those intervals which are found between the notes of the Major scale, or between the notes of either of the forms of the Minor scale, are described as *Diatonic;* while those intervals which can only be found between the notes of the Chromatic scale are described as *Chromatic.* An examination of the intervals formed between the notes of the Harmonic Minor scale, see Ex. 13, will show that such intervals as the Augmented second, the Diminished fourth, the Augmented fifth and the Diminished seventh, although when used in a major key involve the employment of chromatic notes, yet under this general form of classification are correctly described as *Diatonic* intervals :—

Ex. 13.

The interval of the semitone (the smallest interval employed in music) is found in both Diatonic and Chromatic scales. The Diatonic semitone, however, is represented by the employment of two notes of different alphabetical names, as in Ex. 14 (*a*), while the Chromatic semitone is represented by the employment of two notes having the same alphabetical name, one note being inflected by an accidental, as in (*b*) :—

Ex. 14.

Of the intervals which are described as *Chromatic* the most familiar are the Augmented sixth and the Diminished third.

17. **Simple and Compound Intervals.**—A *Simple interval* is one which does not exceed an octave, while a *Compound interval* is larger than an octave, and is made up of an octave added to another interval. The following interval may be described either as a major tenth, or as a Compound major third, because it consists of a major third added to an octave :—

Intervals of the Ninth, Eleventh and Thirteenth, when forming part of the chords bearing these names, must be described as Ninths, Elevenths and Thirteenths, not as Compound seconds, fourths and sixths.

It is difficult to discover what value this form of classification possesses, but while questions referring to it are occasionally to be met with in examination papers, the prospective examinee should bear it in mind.

18.—**Inversion of Intervals.**—To "invert" an interval means to change the relative position of the two notes which form the interval, by placing the lower note above the higher, or the higher note below the lower. If the interval does not exceed an octave, it may be inverted by either note being suitably transposed one octave, as in Ex. 15 (*a*), but if the interval exceeds an octave, the note must be transposed two octaves as in (*b*).

Ex. 15.

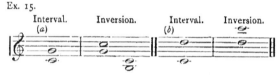

In connection with the inversion of intervals, the chief points to be noted are :—(1) that the numerical value of an interval added to that of its inversion, together, make 9, therefore, if we subtract the numerical value of any interval from 9 we obtain the numerical value of its inversion—thus, the inversion of a unison is an octave, the inversion of a second is a seventh, of a third, a sixth, of a fourth, a fifth, and so on ; (2) that the inversion of a Perfect interval produces a Perfect interval ; (3) that the inversion of a Major interval produces a Minor interval, and the inversion of a Minor interval produces a Major interval ; (4) that the inversion of an Augmented interval produces a Diminished interval, and the inversion of a Diminished interval produces an Augmented interval ; (5) that the inversion of a Consonant interval produces a Consonant interval, and the inversion of a Dissonant interval a Dissonant one. Ex. 16, which shows the inversion of intervals not exceeding an octave, illustrates all these points. The two intervals shown in each bar, the one above and the other below, are inversions of one another.

Ex. 16.

Sixth. – – Augmented. – – – Major. – – – – Minor.

Third. – Diminished. – – – Minor. – – – – Major.

Fifth. – – Augmented. – – – Perfect. – – – Diminished.

Fourth. – Diminished. – – – Perfect. – – – Augmented.

EXERCISES.

1.—Write above each of the following notes a Perfect fourth, a Perfect fifth, a Major second, a Major third, a Major sixth and a Major seventh :—

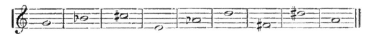

2.—Write above each of the notes given in the previous exercise, Diminished and Augmented fourths, fifths and octaves, Minor and Diminished thirds and sevenths, and Minor and Augmented seconds and sixths.

3 —Write above G sharp in the Treble clef all the Perfect consonances, and above G flat in the Bass clef all the Imperfect consonances.

4.—Write above middle C all the Diatonic intervals, and classify them as Consonant and Dissonant.

5.—Write above and below each of the notes given in Ex. 1 a Chromatic semitone and a Diatonic semitone.

6.—Describe the following intervals and classify them as Diatonic and Chromatic :—

7.—Invert the intervals given above, describe the intervals produced by the inversion, and classify these inversions as Diatonic and Chromatic.

CHAPTER IV.

THE TONIC TRIAD (MAJOR KEY).

19. The simplest complete chord is made up of three different notes, and is formed by adding to any note two others, situated respectively a third and a fifth from it, counting upwards, thus :—

Ex. 17.

The chord thus produced is called a TRIAD. The note from which the intervals are reckoned, that is, the lowest note, is called the *Root* of the triad, and the chord is named after this root. The chord shown above is therefore a triad on C. A diatonic triad may be constructed upon every degree of the major scale, but the most important triad is that upon the Tonic or key-note. The above triad is the Tonic Triad in the key of C major.

20. **Triads and Common Chords.**—Triads are of various kinds according to the nature of the intervals of which they are composed. Those triads in which the fifth is a perfect fifth are generally called COMMON CHORDS, and according as the third from the root is either a major third or a minor third, they are called Major or Minor Common Chords respectively. The Tonic Triad in every major key may therefore be described as a Major Common Chord, because the third note and the fifth note in every major scale are respectively a major third and a perfect fifth from the Tonic or key-note.

21. **Four-part Harmony.**—In Harmony each note of a chord represents what is called "a part." A part is that which is allotted to a single voice in a vocal composition, or to a single instrument in a composition for several instruments (such as a string quartett). Harmony may be written in two parts, in three parts, or in any number of parts up to eight, or even more. For all ordinary purposes, however, the most useful and convenient number of parts is four, and THIS BOOK DEALS ENTIRELY WITH FOUR-PART HARMONY. These four parts will be treated as voice parts, their compass or range corresponding respectively to the compass of the *Soprano, Alto, Tenor* and *Bass voices.* This may be taken approximately as follows :—

Ex. 18.

SOPRANO.　　ALTO.　　TENOR.　　BASS.

Music for these four parts or voices may either be written upon the ordinary Treble and Bass staves, as in Ex. 19, or each part may be written upon a separate staff with the proper clef belonging to that particular voice, as in Ex. 20. In Ex. 19 the parts would be described as being written in "short score," and in Ex. 20 as in "open score." How far the pupil can advantageously employ "open score" when working the various exercises which follow must be decided by the teacher.

Ex. 19.

SOPRANO.

ALTO.

TENOR.

BASS.

Ex. 20.

SOPRANO.
G clef on 2nd line.

ALTO.
C clef on 3rd line.

TENOR.
C clef on 4th line.

BASS.
F clef on 4th line.

22. **The Doubling of Notes.**—In four-part harmony, when dealing with Triads and Common chords, it is necessary, in order to make up the four parts, that one of the notes of the chord should be sounded in two of the parts simultaneously, or in other words should be " doubled." Which notes may be doubled depends upon the nature of the chord. In that under consideration, the Tonic Common Chord in the major key, and *generally in all major common chords, the best note to double is the root,* as in Ex. 21 (*a*), after that comes the fifth, as in (*b*). The third (major) should rarely be doubled, but when it is doubled one of the best distributions of the several notes of the chord is shown at (*c*). It is always possible in a common chord to omit the fifth, and supply the omission by doubling the root twice, as at (*d*), but *the omission of the third,* as at (*e*), *is not allowed.*

Ex. 21.

In all the above chords, the note doubled is always sounded in different octaves, but a note may also be doubled by both parts sounding it at the same pitch, that is, by it being "doubled in the unison." If such a note be a semibreve, this doubling is shown by two semibreves being made to overlap one another, as in the Tenor and Bass parts in Ex. 22 (*a*), while in the case of notes other than semibreves, the doubling is shown by the employment of two stems turned in opposite directions, as in (*b*) :—

Ex. 22.

If the above chords are sounded upon a keyboard instrument they will only produce the effect of three-part Harmony, but this would not be the case if they were sung by voices. Although both the Tenor and Bass voices would sing the same note, yet each would produce a different musical effect, and their combined effect would amount to a distinct doubling of this note.

23. **EAR EXERCISES:**—THE MAJOR COMMON CHORD WITH THE ROOT DOUBLED.—A presentation of the chord *in sound*, in various positions, to be written down by the pupil from dictation, the name of the bass note *only*, being announced to him beforehand.

Ex. 23.

To the Teacher.—Should the pupil find it difficult to discover the notes of which the above chords are composed, they may in the first instance be "spread" after the manner of (*a*). When hearing them for the first time the pupil's attention should be specially directed to the different musical effects of the chords ; *first*, according as the root, the third, or the fifth is at the top, contrasting (*a*), (*b*) and (*c*), and, *secondly*, according as the several notes are situated closely together or in an extended position, contrasting (*a*) with (*d*) and (*b*) with (*e*). The chords in the above exercise should be dictated in various orders, and not merely as they are given above.

THE MAJOR COMMON CHORD WITH THE FIFTH DOUBLED.

Ex. 24.

These chords should be contrasted respectively with (*c*), (*e*) and (*f*) of Ex. 23, and the attention of the pupil directed towards the difference in the musical effect which is created by the doubling of another note in an inner part.

∗ The above Ear Exercises and ALL which follow throughout this
book should be transposed and dictated in other keys, the name of
the key being announced to the pupil beforehand. They should also
be supplemented by other suitable Ear Exercises to be supplied by the
Teacher as such may be required.

24. **The Distribution of Parts**—One of the chief difficulties
in the working of the Exercises which follow this and subsequent
chapters, will be found in securing a good distribution of the notes of a
chord amongst the various vocal parts. These should as far as possible
be made equi-distant from one another, as in Ex. 25 (*a*). In any
progression of chords, however, it is only possible to obtain this to an
approximate degree. When an exceptionally large interval between
two of the parts is necessary it should always lie between the two lowest
parts, as at (*b*), and not between two of the inner parts, as at (*c*), or two
of the upper parts, as at (*d*). In both (*c*) and (*d*) the distribution of
the parts is bad.

Ex. 25.

Good. . . .   Bad . . .

When the three upper notes of a chord are situated so that they do not
extend beyond the compass of an octave, as in Ex. 25 (*b*), the chord is
said to be in "close position," but when they extend beyond an octave,
as in (*a*), the chord is said to be in "extended position."

Although the "close position" and "extended position" of chords is referred to in
nearly every text book upon Harmony, yet we have been unable to discover what
practical value this classification of the position of chords possesses.

25. **The Overlapping of Parts.**—In any progression of chords,
when passing from one chord to the next, no part should proceed to a
higher note than the note in the first chord which belonged to a higher
part, as the Alto does in Ex. 26 (*a*), neither should any part proceed
to a lower note than the note in the first chord which belonged to a
lower part, as the Treble does in (*b*) :—

Ex. 26.

Not good.

As in (*a*) the Alto note of the second chord is higher than the Treble
note of the first chord, and as in (*b*) the Treble note of the second
chord is lower than the Alto note of the first chord, these parts are said
to "overlap." When such overlapping occurs between repetitions of
the same chord it is less objectionable than when it occurs between
different chords, but the pupil would do well in all his early work to
avoid it, except in those instances, hereinafter to be mentioned, in which
it is regarded as unobjectionable (see par. 40).

26 **The Crossing of Parts.**—When a part passes above a higher part, as the Alto of the second chord in Ex 27 (*a*) passes over the Treble, or when a part passes under a lower part, as the Treble of the second chord in (*b*) passes under the Alto, the parts are said "to cross."

Ex 27.

In the working of Harmony exercises *in four parts*, "*crossing of the parts" is not allowed.* Only when some special musical effect is required do composers ever cross their parts in four-part writing.

27. **Mental Conception of Chords.**—When working the Exercises in this book, *'the pupil must always endeavour to realise mentally the sound of every chord as he writes it down.* At first, this may require a considerable mental effort on his part, but by making it a practice *never* to look at a chord written upon paper without trying simultaneously to realise its musical effect, this habit will in time have become so much part of his nature, that such mental conception will eventually require no effort from him, and the sight of a chord represented in notation will immediately create in his mind its sound In connection with this matter, it may be well also to add a word of warning to pupils who are tempted to disregard the above suggestion and to work the exercises in a purely non-musical and mechanical manner, relying upon their knowledge of rules to avoid any bad errors. In the early stages of Harmony, when only a few simple chords are under consideration, it is possible to pursue such a course without revealing one's entire ignorance of the sound of the chords, but the method adopted in this book of employing as exercises, almost entirely unfigured basses and melodies, will soon reveal the deficiencies of the pupil, and unless he alters his method of study, and by systematic ear-training develops his power of musical memory and musical thought up to the level of the chords he is treating upon paper, all real musical progress in Harmony will be at an end

28. In the following Exercises the pupil must not forget that the musical effect of the chords which he is endeavouring mentally to revive will not be that which specially belongs to the Tonic Triad as a *Tonic* chord—but that which is the common property of every Major Common Chord when heard in isolation What we mean is this, the special character of a Major Common Chord as a *Tonic* chord only becomes evident when it is heard in connection with common chords upon other degrees of the scale of which this is the Tonic. Its peculiar function, which is to furnish an effect of final rest or satisfaction, can neither be illustrated nor realised until common chords, which have a totally different musical effect—such as those upon the Dominant and Subdominant—are heard in contrast with it Its consideration in isolation has, however, enabled us to introduce in connection with it various matters, which, while affecting *all* common chords, may, we think, be made simpler by being studied in connection with only one

EXERCISES.

₂ All these and similar Exercises are to be written in four Vocal parts.

1.—Regard each of the following notes as the root of a Tonic Common Chord, prefix to each the key-signature of the Major key, and place over each a Major Common Chord, doubling the root :—

2.—Regard the following notes (1) as roots, (2) as thirds, and (3) as fifths, of Tonic Common Chords, prefix in each case the key-signature of the Major key, and place *under* each a Major Common Chord, doubling the root :—

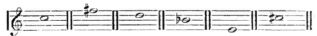

3.—Regard the following notes as fifths of Tonic Common Chords, prefix to each the key-signature of the Major key, and place under each a Major Common Chord, doubling the fifth :—

4.—Harmonize each note of the following Exercises with the Tonic Common Chord of the Major key indicated by the key-signature, treating (a) as Bass parts, (b) as Treble parts, (c) as Alto parts, and (d) as Tenor parts. Either the root or the fifth may be doubled :—

* In these, and in all Bass parts given to be harmonized, in which the same note is repeated, the upper parts should not *necessarily* be repeated in a similar manner. As a general rule the Soprano, and one of the inner parts, should move to other notes of the chord.

CHAPTER V.

THE DOMINANT TRIAD (MAJOR KEY).

29. After the Tonic triad, the next in importance is the triad upon the Dominant or fifth degree of the scale.

Ex. 28.

This, like the Tonic triad, is a Major Common Chord. The third of the Dominant triad being the Leading-Note, this chord is one of exceptional value for defining the key, especially when it is followed by the Tonic common chord, as in the first Ear Exercise. In such cases the Leading-Note, *which may never be doubled* (except under the special conditions mentioned in Chap. XVIII on *Sequences*), almost invariably rises a step to the Tonic.

30. **EAR EXERCISES** UPON THE TONIC AND DOMINANT TRIADS :—

Ex. 29.

The above Exercises may also be dictated in a similar form to that of the first one, where the first chord (the Tonic Triad) is repeated again as the third and final chord.

31. **The Mental Effect of the Dominant Common Chord.**—As the Tonic common chord tends to produce a feeling of *rest*, so the Dominant chord tends to produce one of *unrest*, and when occurring as the penultimate chord of a musical composition, requires to be followed by the Tonic chord, in order that a feeling of satisfaction may be left upon the mind of the listener. If Ex. 30 be played over, and a long pause be made at the rest, only when the final Tonic chord is struck will that sense of finality and completeness, which must characterize the end of a passage, be produced.

C

Ex. 30.

32. The Progression and Movement of Parts.—In the joining of different chords to form harmonic progressions, as is required in the working of the exercises throughout this book, the progression or movement of the several parts in connection with one another has to be carefully considered. It is quite possible for two chords to produce perfectly satisfactory musical effects when heard singly and in isolation, yet when the same two chords are sounded one after the other in close proximity, the progression of the one to the other may produce an effect which, musically speaking, would be considered as bad. In order that faulty progressions may be recognized and avoided by the pupil, rules bearing upon them have been framed from time to time, and the gaining of a knowledge of these and of their application to different kinds of progressions, forms an important part of the study of Harmony. These rules may be divided into two classes, *first*, those which refer to the progression of any single part and are called the rules of MELODIC PROGRESSION; and, *secondly*, those which refer to the progression of two or more parts moving together, and are called the rules of HARMONIC PROGRESSION. The various rules of progression (Melodic and Harmonic), a knowledge of which is required for the working of the exercises at the end of this chapter, will now be introduced. These refer chiefly to Harmonic Progression, and they include many of the most important rules of this class. The other rules of progression will be introduced as the matters to which they specially refer come up, *for the first time*, for consideration.

33. HARMONIC PROGRESSION:—Similar Motion, Contrary Motion, and Oblique Motion.—Any two parts may move in one of three different ways with regard to one another. *First*, they may both move in the same direction as the Soprano and Alto parts move in the first two chords in Ex. 31. They are then said to move in SIMILAR MOTION. *Secondly*, they may move in opposite directions as the Tenor and Bass parts move in the same two chords. They are then said to move in CONTRARY MOTION. *Thirdly*, one part may remain stationary while the other part moves, as the Alto, taken with either of the other parts, does, in the last two chords. In this case, the motion is called OBLIQUE.

Ex. 31.

34. The Motion between the Outside Parts.—The only parts, about the *general motion* of which the pupil need concern himself, are the outside or extreme parts, that is, the Soprano and the Bass. As a rule, Contrary Motion employed between these parts, produces stronger progressions than either Similar Motion or Oblique Motion, and it is therefore in many cases preferable to these. It is, however, impossible without misleading the pupil, to further compare the effects of the employment of different kinds of motion, because either form may be introduced with the best effect by a skilful writer, or with a bad effect by an unskilful one. In ordinary progressions it is not possible to continue any one kind of motion for long, and the best effects are generally produced by a judicious admixture of all three kinds. In this, as in many other matters connected with Harmony, *experience is the only safe guide.*

35. Hidden Octaves and Fifths between the Outside Parts.—When two parts move by Similar Motion to a Perfect octave or a Perfect fifth, such octave or fifth is described as a *Hidden octave* or a *Hidden fifth*, respectively. Hidden octaves and fifths when formed either between two inner parts, or between one inner and one outside part, are (with one important exception to be referred to later on) unobjectionable, but *as a general rule, hidden octaves and fifths formed between the outside parts are not allowed.* There are, however, many exceptions to this rule, and these will be stated as a knowledge of them is required for the correct working of the exercises. Two of the most important of these exceptions will now follow :—

(1) Provided the upper part moves by the step of a second, hidden octaves and fifths between the Tonic and Dominant Triads are allowed, see Ex. 32 (*a*) and (*b*), and

(2) Hidden octaves and fifths formed by a change in the position of the same chord as at (*c*) are allowed.

Ex. 32.

Good.   Good.   Good.   Bad.

Hidden octaves and fifths are sometimes described as "exposed" octaves and fifths, and this term seems to supply a more accurate description of their nature than the traditional one "hidden."

36. Consecutive Unisons, Octaves and Fifths (Similar Motion).—*No two parts (whether outside parts or inner parts) may move in similar motion, in perfect unisons, perfect octaves, or perfect fifths,* see Ex. 33 (*a*), (*b*), and (*c*). Such progressions are generally described simply as *consecutive unisons, consecutive octaves,* and *consecutive fifths* respectively, and are *strictly forbidden.* Repetitions of the same notes, forming between them either of these intervals as at (*d*) are, however, perfectly correct:—

Ex. 33.

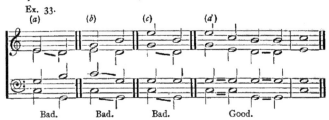

Bad.   Bad.   Bad.   Good.

37. Consecutive Octaves and Fifths (Contrary Motion).—Consecutive octaves and fifths when employed in *contrary motion*, and also the progression from a unison to an octave, or *vice versa*, do not necessarily produce bad musical effects, and such progressions are not strictly forbidden, but even when musically unobjectionable, as in Ex. 34, their employment exhibits a freedom of progression which it should be the prerogative of the advanced student rather than of the beginner to employ, and in all the following exercises they should be avoided.

Ex. 34.

Not bad. .   .   .   .

38. MELODIC PROGRESSION:—Conjunct and Disjunct Movement.—In the framing of progressions composed entirely of Tonic and Dominant Triads (as is required in the immediately following exercises) the opportunities offered for the construction of faulty melodic progressions are few, and, therefore, the more important rules belonging to this class will not be introduced till later, when the pupil's harmonic resources have been increased, and with them his opportunities for framing incorrect parts. Although there are no special rules of melodic progression which he is likely to infringe in the individual parts of the simple progressions he is now about to construct, yet it is upon the general nature and flow of these parts that the smooth movement of one chord to the next, so desirable in such progressions, almost entirely depends. This smoothness of progression is largely obtained by letting each note forming an upper part of a chord move to the note in the next chord which is nearest to it, provided such movement does not infringe any of the rules of harmonic progression already mentioned, see Ex. 35 (*a*). When the movement is made by the step of the second, as in the Soprano of Ex. 35, it is called *Conjunct Movement,* but when a larger interval is employed, as in the Bass of the same example, it is called *Disjunct*

Movement. In progressions of chords, if a note is common to two or more adjacent chords, the part in which this note appears should remain stationary, that is, the note should be repeated, as in the Alto of (*a*). In the following examples where the Bass part is assumed as given to be harmonized, the smoothness of the progression in (*a*) is unmistakable, and on that ground alone would make the arrangement of the parts in (*a*) preferable to that given in (*b*) :—

Ex. 35.

Good.   Not good.

39. **Progression of the Leading-Note,** and **Omission of the Fifth in a Tonic Common Chord.**—In progressions in which the Tonic Triad is preceded by the Dominant Triad, and the Soprano part is formed by the fifth of the Dominant (the Supertonic) falling to the Tonic, as in Ex. 36 (*a*), (*b*), in order that the Leading-note may rise to the Tonic, the fifth of the Tonic chord is generally omitted and the root doubled twice, as in Ex. 36 (*a*). It is, however, not incorrect, although less usual, for the Leading-note to fall a third to the fifth of the Tonic chord, as in (*b*). The pupil as a general rule should make all his Leading-notes rise, unless they occur in a descending scale passage, or in a repetition of the same chord, as in (*c*).

Ex. 36.

40. **Allowable Overlapping of Parts.**—In progressions formed of Tonic and Dominant Triads, when the root is doubled in the unison to represent both the Tenor and the Bass parts, as in Ex. 37, the overlapping of parts caused by the root of the Tonic chord proceeding to the root and third of the Dominant chord, or *vice-versa*, as shown below, is unobjectionable.

Ex. 37.

Good.

41. The Harmonization of Basses and Melodies.—In the working of the Exercises the following points should be borne in mind :—

(1). Every Exercise must *end* with the Tonic chord. The large majority of Exercises also begin with the Tonic chord, but a few later on will be found to begin with the Dominant chord.

(2). In the construction of a melody over a given Bass part, the *first* note of the melody may be either of the notes of the first chord, but the *last* note of the melody should generally be the Tonic itself. A melody may however end upon the Mediant (the third of the Tonic chord), but it should not end upon the Dominant (the fifth of the Tonic chord).

(3). The outside parts should, if possible, move in contrary motion, and in order to admit of this a melody (or bass) which begins upon a high note and proceeds generally in a downward direction, should be harmonized with a bass part (or melody) which begins upon a low note and proceeds generally in an upward direction, and *vice versa*.

(4). The fifth of a common chord may be omitted and the root doubled twice, whenever the progression of the parts can thereby be improved.

EXERCISES.

Harmonize the following Bass parts and Treble parts with Tonic and Dominant Common chords :—

CHAPTER VI.

THE SUBDOMINANT TRIAD (MAJOR KEY).

42. After the Tonic and Dominant Triads, the next in importance is the Triad upon the Subdominant or fourth degree of the scale, which is also a Major Common Chord.

Ex. 38.

EAR EXERCISES UPON THE TONIC AND SUBDOMINANT TRIADS :—

Ex. 39.

Each of the above progressions may also be dictated in a similar form to that of the first one. After the pupil has become somewhat familiar with the sound of them, they should be contrasted in sound with the corresponding progressions formed by the Tonic and Dominant Triads, par. 30.

43. **Hidden Octaves and Fifths.**—As in progressions of Tonic and Dominant Triads, so in progressions of Tonic and Subdominant Triads, hidden octaves and fifths are freely allowed between the outside parts, provided the upper part moves by the step of a second as in Ex. 40.

Ex. 40.

Good.

For the working of the following Exercises, with the above exception, no further rules of progression are required, beyond those which have already been given in the previous chapters, and which apply to all chords except where it is otherwise stated.

EXERCISES.

Harmonize the following Bass parts and Treble parts with Tonic and Subdominant Common Chords :—

CHAPTER VII.

THE THREE PRIMARY TRIADS (MAJOR KEY).

44. The three Triads which we have now considered, the Tonic Triad, the Dominant Triad, and the Subdominant Triad, are the only major triads or major common chords which can be formed from the notes of the major scale, and they are called the PRIMARY TRIADS of the key. They are so-called because of their great importance in defining the key, the notes of which they are formed including every note in the scale, and a knowledge of them therefore supplies the pupil with sufficient harmonic resources to harmonize the complete major scale, thus :—

Ex. 41.

45. **The Selection of Chords** in the Harmonization of Melodies.—The above harmonization of the several notes of the scale is the only possible one with these three triads, when the notes of the scale are employed in a regular and continuous progression, either ascending or descending, but in suitable melodic progressions it is also possible to harmonize the note C—the Tonic—with the Subdominant Triad as Ex. 42 (*a*), and the note G—the Dominant—with the Dominant Triad as in (*b*), instead of harmonizing them with the Tonic Triad as in the above example :—

Ex. 42.

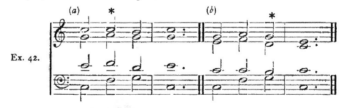

In many of the melodies for harmonization given at the end of this chapter a choice of two chords will frequently be possible in harmonizing the Tonic and the Dominant. In such cases the pupil will have to decide which is the more suitable chord to employ, and he will only be able to do so with certainty and success if he can create in his mind the musical effect which either chord would produce in each particular instance.

46. **EAR EXERCISES**:—

Ex. 43.

Strictly speaking, the only new feature presented by the employment of these three triads, is the progression formed by the Subdominant Triad proceeding to the Dominant Triad, and *vice versa*, the Dominant Triad proceeding to the Subdominant Triad. The former of these progressions, the Subdominant Triad to the Dominant Triad, is a far more useful and satisfactory progression than the latter, the Dominant Triad to the Subdominant Triad. This latter must be employed with great care, otherwise a harsh and unmusical effect will be produced. A good arrangement of the several notes of the chords is shown in the fourth Ear Exercise given above. If the progressions formed of these two chords are to be made correctly, several new and important rules of Melodic Progression must now be stated.

47. **MELODIC PROGRESSION**:—**Augmented Intervals in Melody.**—*No part may proceed by an Augmented interval unless both of the notes forming the interval belong to the same chord.* The only Augmented interval with which we are at present concerned is the Augmented fourth, formed between the Subdominant and the Leading-note of the Major scale, reckoned upwards. In the key of C this would be as follows :—

Ex. 44.

These two notes, when forming this interval, may not follow one another in any part, unless they are both harmonized by the same chord. As at present they can only be harmonized by two different chords, the Subdominant by the Subdominant Triad, and the Leading-note by the Dominant Triad; their employment as adjacent notes, so as to form this interval, is strictly forbidden.

48. **Diminished Intervals in Melody.**—*When a part proceeds by a Diminished interval, it must immediately return to a note within that interval.* The only diminished interval with which we are at present concerned is the Diminished fifth which lies between the

Leading-note and the Subdominant of the scale, reckoned upwards. This Diminished fifth is the inversion of the Augmented fourth mentioned in the previous paragraph. Whenever the two notes which form this fifth are employed in a part as adjacent notes, the note which follows must be a note lying within their compass, thus:—

Ex. 45.

Good.   Not good.

49. **Large Intervals in Melody.**—*When an interval larger than a sixth is employed in any part, it should be approached and quitted in the opposite direction to which the leap is made,* thus:—

Ex. 46.

Good.   Not good.

*A part should not proceed by the interval of a seventh unless both of the notes forming the interval belong to the same chord.** Until the chord of the seventh is reached it is therefore not possible to employ the interval of the seventh between adjacent notes. In connection with triads, this interval should only be employed in any part when there are not less than two notes between those forming the seventh, unless there be a leap of an octave as in (*b*). Such a Bass part as shown in (*a*) must be carefully avoided:—

(*a*)   (*b*)

Ex. 47.

Not good.   Good.

50. **Progression of the Subdominant Triad to the Dominant Triad.**—When proceeding from the Subdominant Triad to the Dominant Triad and *vice versa*, special care will be required in order to avoid consecutive octaves and fifths being formed between the two triads, as in Ex. 48 (*a*). In progressions of these two chords, the parts which in the first chord contain the fifth and the octave of the Root must move in contrary motion to the Bass, as in (*b*). The hidden fifth, as illustrated in (*c*), is of course incorrect.

(*a*)   (*b*)   (*c*)

Ex. 48.

Bad.   Good.   Bad.

* An exception to this rule sometimes occurs in the Minor key in connection with the Diminished Seventh (see par. 71).

51. Final Cadences.—The last two chords in a piece of music form what is called the CLOSE or FINAL CADENCE, the second of the two chords being always the Tonic Common Chord in its root position. Although only three different triads have been considered, yet two of the most important "final cadences" may be formed from these. Thus, if the Tonic Triad be preceded by the Dominant Triad to form the concluding chords, an *Authentic or Perfect Cadence* is formed, while if the Tonic Triad be preceded by the Subdominant Triad, a *Plagal Cadence* is formed. Of the Ear Exercises in Ex. 43, the first three end with Perfect Cadences and the last with a Plagal Cadence.

52. **Ear Exercises.**—The teacher should test the pupil's power of discriminating these different forms of cadence by playing such in various keys.

EXERCISES.

Harmonize the following Basses and Melodies employing the three Primary Triads :—

CHAPTER VIII.

THE THREE PRIMARY TRIADS (MINOR KEY).

53. As in the major key, the Primary Triads in the minor key are those formed upon the Tonic, the Dominant and the Subdominant, and we shall consider them in the same order as we did in the major key.

54. **The TONIC TRIAD in the Minor key** is made up of a Minor third and a Perfect fifth from the root, as shown below, and is therefore a Minor Common Chord (see par. 20):—

In this chord the best note to double is the root, but in this and *in all Minor Common Chords, either the third or the fifth may be doubled instead of the root,* if desired.

55. **Ear Exercises :—**

THE MINOR COMMON CHORD WITH THE ROOT DOUBLED.

Ex. 49.

WITH THE FIFTH DOUBLED.　　WITH THE THIRD DOUBLED.

The above chords should be severally contrasted *in sound* with corresponding major common chords (par. 23), so that the pupil may learn to recognise, readily, either major or minor chords by their sound.

56. **The "Tierce de Picardie."**—In former times it was the custom to bring a composition in a Minor key to a close, by employing as the final chord, the Major Common Chord upon the key-note, instead

of the Minor Common Chord, which Major chord was called the
"*Tierce de Picardie.*" This practice is not a common one amongst
modern composers, and it is now almost entirely confined to church
music.

57. **The DOMINANT TRIAD in the Minor key** is
composed of exactly the same notes as that in the major key and is
therefore a Major Common Chord.

Ex. 50.

As the third of the Dominant Triad is the Leading-note, it must always
be modified by an accidental in a similar manner to the Leading-note
of the key to which it belongs. The conditions as to the doubling of
the notes of the Dominant Triad in the Minor key are the same as
those which apply to the notes of the Dominant chord in the Major
key. The root is the best note to double. The third may *never* be
doubled.

58. **Ear Exercises** UPON THE TONIC AND DOMINANT TRIADS.—
Before proceeding to the following Exercises, the Ear Exercises upon
the same chords in the Major key (Ex. 29) should be transposed and
dictated in the key of C minor, and also in other Minor keys:—

Ex. 51.

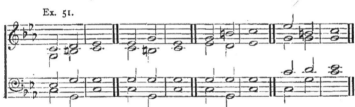

59. **Melodic Progression.**—In progressions of these two triads
in the Minor key, the formation, in the same part, of the interval of an
Augmented fifth or of its inversion, the Diminished fourth, becomes
possible. The Augmented fifth, which is formed between the third of
the Tonic chord and the third of the Dominant chord, Ex. 52 (*a*), must
be avoided altogether. When the Diminished fourth (the inversion of
the same notes) occurs, the next note in that part must return to a
note within the fourth, as in (*b*), and not proceed to a note outside the
interval, as in (*c*):—

Ex. 52.
(*a*)   (*b*)   (*c*)

Bad.   Good.   Bad.

As in the Major key, the Leading-note almost invariably rises a step to
the Tonic.

EXERCISES.

Harmonize the following with Tonic and Dominant Common Chords :—

60. The SUBDOMINANT TRIAD in the Minor Key, like the Tonic Triad in the Minor key, is a Minor Common Chord :—

With regard to the best notes to double in this triad, see par. 54.

Ear Exercises UPON THE TONIC AND SUBDOMINANT TRIADS.— Before proceeding to the following Exercises, the Ear Exercises upon the same chords in the Major key (Ex. 39) should be transposed and dictated in the key of C minor, and also in other Minor keys.

EXERCISES.

Harmonize the following with Tonic and Subdominant Common Chords :—

61. The **THREE PRIMARY TRIADS** in the Minor Key.

Ear Exercises:—

Ex. 55.

The chief difficulties presented by the employment in the Minor key of the three Primary Triads are those of melodic progression. In addition to the Augmented fourth formed between the Subdominant and Leading-note, Ex. 56 (*a*) (as in the Major key), there are two other Augmented intervals which can be formed by the progression of the Subdominant Triad to the Dominant Triad. One is the Augmented second between the sixth and seventh degrees of the Harmonic Minor Scale, shown at (*b*), and the other is the Augmented fourth between the sixth degree and the second degree of the same scale, reckoning upwards as shown at (*c*):—

Ex. 56.

(*a*)   (*b*)   (*c*)

Bad.   Bad.   Bad.

At the present stage of advancement *all such melodic progressions must be carefully avoided.*

EXERCISES.

Harmonize the following, employing the three Primary Triads:—

CHAPTER IX.

THE PRIMARY TRIADS IN THEIR FIRST INVERSION.

62. Common Chords and their Inversions.—A common chord which is heard with its root as the lowest note is said to be in its *original position* or its *root position.* All the chords we have hitherto considered have been heard, only in their root position. When, however, the notes of a chord are so arranged that the root is not sounded as the lowest note but appears only in the upper parts, the chord is said to be in *an inverted form*, or merely *an inversion.* Thus, in the following example the first chord is the common chord of C in its original or root position, while the second and third chords are inversions of it :—

Ex. 57.

A chord has the same number of inversions as the number of notes which make up the chord, omitting the root, and they are generally described as first inversion, second inversion, and so on, according to the position of their bass note in the original position of the chord. Thus, the first inversion is that which has the third of the original chord as its bass note, as in Ex. 57 (*b*), and the second inversion is that which has the fifth of the original chord as its bass note, as in (*c*).

63. The TONIC and DOMINANT TRIADS—First Inversion.

Ear Exercises :—

Ex. 58.

*** The above Ear Exercises should be transposed into the key of C minor, and dictated in that key as well as in the Major key.

D

64. **The Mental Effect of Triads in their First Inversion.**—The effect left upon the mind by the first inversion of a triad, compared with the effect of the same triad heard in its original position, is one of much less strength and firmness. Whilst retaining its own special musical character (that is, as a Tonic, Dominant, Subdominant, or whatever chord it may be) that character is less strongly defined. Yet it is because of the existence of such differences of musical effect between the root position and the inversions of a triad, that we are able by a judicious employment of different positions of the same chord to obtain a varied and pleasing harmonization of a melody without too frequently changing the chord. The two harmonizations of the same phrase, shown in Ex. 59, will illustrate this point. In (a) the effect is one of strength but also of monotony, the chords being in their strongest position upon both the strong and the weak beats of the bar. In (b) the variety and interest of the musical effect has been largely increased by the employment of first inversions upon the weaker beats of the bar :—

Ear Exercises:—

Ex. 59.

It must not be inferred from this that the inversions of triads are always most effective when employed upon the weak beats of a bar, and the root position of triads when employed upon the strong beats. No general rule of this kind is possible, for it is quite easy to give examples in which such would not be the case. The only guides to an effective employment of the different positions of a chord are, *first*, a knowledge of their respective musical effects, and, *secondly*, the experience gained by the framing of many progressions in which such are included.

65. **The Doubling of Notes.**—In the first inversion of common chords, the same notes may be doubled as in the original position. In both major and minor common chords, therefore, either the root may be doubled, as in Ex 60 (a) and (c), or the fifth from the root, as in (b) and (d). These in a first inversion are the sixth and the third from the bass note respectively. In the first inversion of a minor common chord, the bass note, the third of the chord in its original position may also be doubled, as in (e) :—

Ex. 60.

Root C   .   .   .   .

66. The Figuring of Chords: Figured Basses.—In the study of Harmony a method of indicating the various chords in a more concise manner than by writing them in full upon a staff, is frequently a great convenience, if not an absolute necessity. For this purpose a system has been gradually built up, by which the notes of a chord may be indicated by figures placed one above another, under the bass note of the chord, showing numerically the intervals at which the several notes of the chord are distant from this bass note. A bass part under which the chords by which it is to be harmonised are indicated in this manner, is called a *Figured Bass*. In Figured Basses, notes which are to be harmonized by triads in their original position are left unfigured. The only exception to this rule is when either of the notes of a triad require an accidental, as, for instance, the third of the Dominant chord in the Minor key. In such cases a ♯, ♭ or ♮, whichever is necessary to effect the required change, should be placed under the bass note, as in Ex. 61. This means that the *third* of the triad upon this note is to be modified in accordance with the accidental.

Ex. 61.

When it is required to modify any other interval, an accidental indicating the nature of the inflection must be placed before the figure representing the note to be inflected, as ♭5 or ♯6, which mean respectively, that the fifth from the bass should be flattened, or the sixth from the bass sharpened. A line drawn through a figure, thus ⑥, indicates that the note represented by the figure is to be raised a semitone. The first inversion of triads, having a third and a sixth from the bass note, would if completely figured be represented by ⁶₃, this however is abbreviated to 6, the 3 being implied, as illustrated in Ex. 62, and these chords are frequently described as "*chords of the sixth.*"

Ex. 62.

The figuring of the various chords, where this requires further explanation, will be considered as each chord is introduced for study.

EXERCISES.

*** In these, and in ALL similar Exercises which follow, the Pupil should, after he has worked an exercise, figure the Bass in accordance with the chords (root position or inversion) which he has employed. He should also write the Root of each chord upon a separate staff (under the Bass staff), left blank for this special purpose.

Harmonize the following, employing Tonic and Dominant Triads in their root position and first inversion :—

67. The **SUBDOMINANT TRIAD.** First Inversion.
Ear Exercises:—

Ex. 63.

*** To be dictated also in C minor.

EXERCISES.

Harmonize the following, employing Tonic and Subdominant Triads in their root position and first inversion :—

68. **The THREE PRIMARY TRIADS. First Inversion.**

Ear Exercises:—

Ex. 64.

(Also in C minor).

69. **The Doubling of Notes in Chords of the Sixth.—**
In progressions of chords of the sixth upon adjacent bass notes, as
illustrated by the progression of the first inversion of the Subdominant
Triad to the first inversion of the Dominant Triad, care must be taken
to avoid the formation of such consecutive fifths or octaves between
the upper parts as are shown in Ex. 65 (*a*). Thus, when the fifth
of the original chord is placed above the root, as in the treble and
alto of the first chord of (*a*), the parts containing these notes must not
move conjunctly to the fifth and root of the next chord respectively,
otherwise consecutive fifths will be formed; neither must the corresponding note in both chords (the fifth or the root), be doubled in the
same parts, as in the Treble and Tenor of (*a*), otherwise consecutive
octaves will be formed. Such incorrect progressions may be avoided
by doubling different notes in each chord, that is, the root in one
chord and the fifth in the other, as in (*b*), and also by the employment
of contrary motion, as in (*c*) :—

Ex. 65.

70. **The Doubling of the Third in Major Common
Chords.**—Although as a general rule the third of a Major Common
Chord should not be doubled (whether such chord be in its Root
position or in an inverted form), yet such doubling is allowed provided
both notes are approached and quitted by step in opposite directions,
as is the third of the Subdominant Triad in Ex. 66.

Ex. 66.

Good

71. The Minor Seventh in the Minor key as a Bass note.—In the minor key the progression of the first inversion of the Dominant Triad to either the first inversion of the Subdominant Triad, or the root position of the Submediant Triad (or *vice versa*), is inadmissible, because of the interval of the Augmented Second which would be formed between the two bass notes thus :—

Ex. 67.
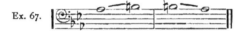

In order to avoid this interval, when the bass part *descends* stepwise from the Tonic to the Submediant, the descending form of the Melodic Minor Scale may be employed, that is, the Minor Seventh (B flat in the key of C minor) may be substituted for the Major Seventh (B natural) and like that note, harmonized with a $\frac{6}{3}$ chord, as in Ex. 68.

Ear Exercise :—

Ex. 68.

The Minor Seventh is available as a bass note only in passages which *descend* from the Tonic to the Submediant. It is *not* available in corresponding passages which *ascend*. A chord upon the Leading-note sometimes follows one upon the Submediant by the bass leaping a Diminished Seventh downwards as in Ex. 69, but such a progression should *not* be employed at this early stage.

Ear Exercise :—

Ex. 69.

EXERCISES.

Harmonize the following, employing the three Primary Triads in their root position and first inversion :—

In the following Exercises the "chord of the sixth" upon the Minor Seventh of the scale is to be introduced at each of the places indicated *.

CHAPTER X.

THE SUBMEDIANT TRIAD.

73. There yet remain four diatonic triads to be considered, those upon the *Submediant*, the *Supertonic*, the *Mediant* and the *Leading-note*. To distinguish these from the Primary Triads, they are sometimes called SECONDARY TRIADS. The most useful and familiar of the Secondary Triads is the Submediant Triad, which we shall consider next.

74. *In the Major key*, the triad upon the Submediant, or sixth degree of the scale, is a Minor Common Chord, see Ex. 70 (*a*). It is therefore unlike either of the other triads in that key which we have yet considered, all having been Major Common Chords. *In the Minor key*, the Submediant Triad is a Major Common Chord, see Ex. (*b*).

Ex. 70.

75. **EAR EXERCISES (Root Position).**—In connection with the study of the following Ear Exercises, the pupil, after endeavouring to write down from dictation each series, should carefully read the statement which follows, and which has been added for his guidance when harmonizing the basses and melodies upon this chord. It will be excellent practice for him to test the accuracy of these several statements, by a further study of the same chords placed in a different order and with the parts differently arranged :—

Ex. 71.

*** To be dictated also in C minor.

I. *Progressions formed of the Submediant Triad and either of the Primary Triads (or vice versa), both chords being in their root position, are almost invariably good.* The least satisfactory is that formed by the Submediant Triad proceeding to the Tonic Triad, thus :—

Ex. 72.

Weak.

When either the Tonic Triad or the Subdominant Triad is followed by the Submediant Triad, as indicated by the bass parts given in Ex. 73, it is better for the bass to leap a third, as in (a), than a sixth, as in (b). The leap of a sixth in a bass which is harmonized by triads in their root position, frequently produces a weak effect :—

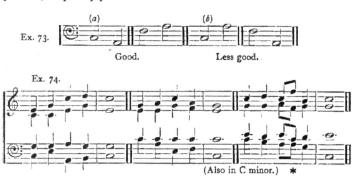

Ex. 73.

(a)   (b)

Good.   Less good.

Ex. 74.

(Also in C minor.)   ✳

II. *Progressions formed of the Submediant Triad in its root position, and either of the Primary Triads in their first inversion, are mostly good.* Such progressions naturally lack the strength of the last mentioned ones, in which chords in their root position only, were employed. This will be specially noticeable in progressions formed of the Submediant Triad and the first inversion of the Subdominant Triad, where both chords have the same bass note. In this, and in most progressions of triads and their inversions where the bass note is repeated, it is better for the second chord to be upon a weaker beat (as in Ex. 75) or upon the weaker part of a beat (as in Ex. 74 ✳), than the first chord, and also for the treble part to move, that is, not to repeat the same note.

Ex. 75.

✳

76. The Harmonization of Basses and Melodies.—
The introduction of the Submediant Triad, adds very considerably to
the pupil's harmonic resources in both major and minor keys. *In the
Major key* it brings within his range an entirely new element of contrast
in the form of a *Minor* Common Chord, and either of the three notes
of which it is composed, and which he has hitherto been compelled to
harmonize with a major chord, he is now able to harmonize with either
a major chord or a minor chord, as in Ex. 76 (*a*). *In the Minor key* it is
capable of similar employment, but with an opposite musical effect, for
it enables the pupil to harmonize either of its three notes, which have
hitherto been necessarily harmonized with a minor chord, with either a
minor chord or a major chord, as in (*b*) :—

Ex. 76.

Major Triads. Minor Triad. Minor Triads. Major Triad.

With increased resources however comes increased responsibility, for
as there are now two and sometimes three different chords, either of
which it may be possible to employ, to harmonize a note in a given
bass or melody, such harmonization requires a constant exercise of the
pupil's taste and judgment, in order that the most suitable chord may
be employed in each particular instance. This selection of suitable
chords will naturally tend to become more difficult, as the resources of
the pupil are enlarged, by the introduction to him of further new chords,
but, provided he *memorizes the sound of each chord before he makes use of
it in written exercises*, and is able to hear, mentally, the musical effect
of what he is writing down, the difficulties of selection will gradually
disappear.

77. The Doubling of Notes.—*In the Major key*, the Submediant
Triad being a Minor Common Chord, either the root, the third, or the fifth
may be doubled. It will frequently be found that a better arrangement
of the parts may be obtained by doubling the third, and this may be done
without any hesitation, see Ex. 71 (*b*) and (*c*). *In the Minor key,* this Triad
being a Major Common Chord, according to the general rule, either the
root or the fifth should be doubled; when, however, it is either preceded
or followed by the Dominant Triad, it forms an exception to this rule and
the third is usually doubled. The reasons for this exceptional course
are not difficult to discover. Assuming, for example, that the Dominant
Triad precedes the Submediant Triad, as in Ex. 77, the third of the
Dominant Triad (the Leading-note) naturally rises a step to the third of
the Submediant Triad (the Tonic) ; if, then, the fifth of the Dominant
Triad also rises a step to the fifth of the Submediant, as in (*a*), consecu-

tive fifths are formed with the bass, or if the fifth of the Dominant chord leaps downward to the root of the Submediant chord, as in (*b*), an augmented fourth is formed in that part. Both of these progressions are incorrect. It only remains then for the fifth of the Dominant chord to fall a second to the third of the Submediant chord, thus doubling the third, as in (*c*). This is by far the best, as well as the most familiar arrangement of the parts. The exceptional leaping of the Leading-note a diminished fourth, as in (*d*), provided the next Tenor note is a note within this interval, is a possible progression, but it will be found a far less useful one than that shown in (*c*).

Ex. 77.

78. **The "Interrupted Cadence."**—The progression of the Dominant Triad to the Submediant Triad is frequently employed to form what is called the "*Interrupted Cadence*." The Interrupted Cadence is one of the most important of the MIDDLE CADENCES, so called, because they can only occur during the progress of a composition and never at the end. In the following exercises, an Interrupted Cadence should be introduced at each of the places marked (*a*).

Ear Exercises.—The teacher should test the pupil's power of discriminating by their sound, Perfect, Plagal, and Interrupted Cadences, by playing such in various keys.

EXERCISES.

Harmonize the following, introducing the Submediant Triad at each of the places indicated :—

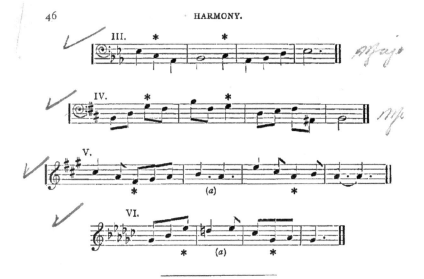

79. The FIRST INVERSION of the SUBMEDIANT TRIAD.

Ear Exercises:—

Ex. 78.

(Also in C minor.)   (Also in C minor.)

In this inversion, the Bass note is generally the best note to double, although either of the other notes may be doubled, if desired.

The progressions formed of the first inversion of the Submediant Triad and either of the Primary Triads are, taken as a whole, far less useful than those formed when the Submediant Triad is in its root position. Progressions formed of the first inversion of the Submediant Triad and either of the Primary Triads in their root position, are, in general, less satisfactory than progressions in which the Primary Triads are present in their first inversion. In progressions of the former class, when the Tonic Triad is employed, as in Ex. 78 (a), the pupil should remember what was said in par. 75, with reference to a repeated bass note.

EXERCISES.

Harmonize the following, introducing the first inversion of the Submediant Triad at each of the places indicated :—

CHAPTER XI.

THE SUPERTONIC TRIAD.

80. *In the Major key*, the triad on the Supertonic or second degree of the scale is a Minor Common Chord, see Ex. 79 (*a*). *In the Minor key*, the fifth from the Supertonic being a Diminished fifth and the third a Minor third, the triad which is formed upon this note is called a Diminished triad, see Ex. 79 (*b*) :—

Ex. 79.

As a Diminished triad is what is called a "discord," and its progression is subject to certain restrictions, its consideration will be postponed until after all the concords have been introduced (Chap. XVI), and we shall confine our attention (so far as the root position of the Supertonic triad is concerned), to the Supertonic Triad in the Major key. Either of the notes of this chord may be doubled when it is employed in the Major key, but a better progression of parts will often be obtained by doubling the third instead of the root or the fifth.

81. **EAR EXERCISES (Root Position)**:—

Ex. 80.

The progressions formed of the Supertonic Triad and either of the other triads of the key which have already been considered, differ so greatly, both in usefulness and musical effect, that they require to be referred to separately.

I. The Supertonic Triad used in connection with the Tonic Triad or its first inversion.—As there is no note which is common to these two chords (Tonic and Supertonic Triads), such progressions are characterised by an absence of smoothness, which, if care be not exercised in the arrangement of the several parts, may amount to definite harshness.   At the same time, provided the parts be judiciously distributed and the outside parts move in contrary motion, such progressions may, with one exception, be employed with good effect, see Ex. 80 (*a*) and (*d*).   The exception is the progression of the Supertonic Triad to the Tonic Triad, when both chords are in their root position, thus :—

Ex. 81.

This progression should be avoided.

II. The Dominant Triad or its first inversion.—The effect of progressions formed of Supertonic and Dominant Triads is almost invariably excellent.   The roots of these triads being situated a fourth apart (or a fifth apart, whichever chord comes first), the chords stand in a somewhat similar relationship to one another as the Tonic Triad to the Subdominant Triad (or the Dominant Triad), and this is the strongest relative position which any two triads can occupy.   In progressions formed of these two chords, even when such hidden fifths occur as are shown below, the musical effect is nearly always good.

Ex. 82.

Good.

One of the most familiar positions of the Supertonic Triad, is when it precedes the Dominant chord (or the second inversion of the Tonic chord) in leading up to a Cadence, see Ex. 80 (*b*), (*c*) and (*d*), also Ex. 95 (*c*).

III. The Subdominant Triad or its first inversion.—Of progressions which may be formed of Supertonic and Subdominant Triads, the strongest is that in which the Subdominant Triad precedes the Supertonic Triad, both chords being in their root position and the bass leaping a third downwards, as in Ex. 80 (*b*).   Other progressions formed of these chords may be used, but with the exception of the one shown in (*e*), none of them are very strong.

IV. THE SUBMEDIANT TRIAD OR ITS FIRST INVERSION.—The roots
of these two triads (Supertonic and Submediant) being situated a fifth
apart (or a fourth apart, whichever chord comes first) the musical effect
of progressions formed of these chords is almost invariably good, see
Ex. 80 (c) and (e).

EXERCISES.

Harmonize the following, introducing the Supertonic Triad at each of
the places indicated :—

**82. The FIRST INVERSION of the SUPERTONIC
TRIAD.**—Although the Supertonic Triad in its root position in the
minor key, having a dissonant interval (a diminished fifth) from the
bass, is unavailable for employment as a common chord, yet in its first
inversion, when the dissonant interval (the augmented fourth or its inversion the diminished fifth) occurs only between two of the upper parts,
as in Ex. 83 (b) and (c), it may be employed with the same freedom as
the first inversion in the major key :—

Ear Exercises (To be dictated also in C minor):—

Ex. 83.

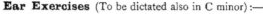

Progressions formed of the first inversion of the Supertonic Triad and either of the triads previously considered, in their root position, are generally good (see (*a*), (*c*) and (*d*)), except that in which the Sub-dominant triad is employed, when, the bass being repeated, the musical effect is weak. Progressions in which both the chords are employed in their first inversion lack strength, but if judiciously introduced, may produce good, and even excellent effects, see (*b*).

83. **Progressions formed of a Perfect Fifth and a Diminished Fifth.**—In the minor key, the progression of a common chord (root position or inversion) to the first inversion of the diminished triad upon the Supertonic (or *vice versa*), makes the progression of a perfect fifth, followed or preceded by a diminished fifth, possible, as shown in Ex. 84. Progressions like these, formed of fifths of two different kinds, obviously do not produce the same effect as progressions formed of two perfect fifths, and are not, like them, universally prohibited. When a progression formed of a perfect fifth and a diminished fifth occurs between two upper parts, (as such fifths only can occur at the present stage), provided the perfect fifth comes first, as shown in (*a*), it is freely allowed; while, when the diminished fifth comes first, as in (*b*), it is also allowed, if either of the parts forming the fifths move by the step of a semitone. A much better progression, however, is formed when the lower part rises a semitone, as will be shown in connection with the first inversion of the Leading-note Triad, Ex. 92 (*b*), than when the higher part falls a semitone, as in Ex. 84 (*b*). It will be better for the pupil to avoid such a progression as (*b*) in his early exercises:—

Ex. 84.

E

EXERCISES.

Harmonize the following, introducing the first inversion of the Supertonic Triad at each of the places indicated :—

Harmonize the following in accordance with the figuring :—

CHAPTER XII.

THE MEDIANT TRIAD.

84. *In the Major key*, the triad on the Mediant or third degree of the scale, is a Minor Common Chord, see Ex. 85 (*a*). *In the Minor key*, the fifth from the Mediant being an augmented fifth, and the third a major third, the triad which is formed upon this note is called an Augmented triad, see Ex. 85 (*b*) :—

Ex. 85.

The Augmented triad is a discord and will be considered with the other dissonant triads in Chap. XVI. In this chapter we shall confine our attention, so far as the root position of this triad is concerned, to the Mediant triad in the Major key. Either the root or the third of the chord may be doubled, but the fifth (the Leading-note) may not be doubled.

85. Ear Exercises (Root Position):—

Ex. 86.

The triad upon the Mediant is the least useful of the common chords in the Major key, and, unless great care be exercised in its employment, unsatisfactory and harsh progressions will be produced. Some of the progressions formed of this triad and the Subdominant Triad in its root position being amongst the most unsatisfactory of these. When the Mediant Triad is used in connection with the Submediant Triad or its first inversion, the effect is generally excellent, and there are a few other chords, (some of which are shown above), with which it may be employed, also with good effect. Its employment, however, should be rare, except in those exercises in which it is specially indicated.

EXERCISES.

Harmonize the following, introducing the Mediant Triad at each of
the places indicated :—

86. The FIRST INVERSION of the MEDIANT
TRIAD. As in the first inversion of the Mediant Triad in the Minor
key, the dissonant interval (the diminished fourth, or its inversion,
the augmented fifth) occurs only between two of the upper parts, see
Ex. 87 (*b*) and (*c*), this chord, in its first inversion, is available for
unrestricted employment in both major and minor keys.

Ex. 87.

87. **Ear Exercises** (to be dictated also in C minor) :—

Ex. 88.

This inversion, like the root position of the same chord, is not frequently
used, but it may be employed with excellent effect when followed either
by the Dominant, Tonic, or Submediant Triad, as shown above. The
best effect is produced when the root of the chord is in the highest part

and the bass note is doubled, as in the last four Ear Exercises. When employed in this form in Cadences, it is frequently described as a *chord of the Dominant Thirteenth*, and as such it will be fully considered in the chapter upon the Chord of the Dominant Thirteenth (Part II).

88. The Harmonization of Figured Basses.—In the harmonization of Exercises XI and XII, and of all subsequent figured basses, the pupil should bear in mind the two following points:— (1) When a line is placed immediately under a bass note, it means that the chord over the previous bass note is to be either repeated or sustained over this bass note, as in Ex. 89 (*a*). (2) When a line is used in connection with a figure, as in (*b*), it means that the note indicated by the figure or accidental which immediately precedes the line, is to be repeated or sustained to the end of the line. Thus, the B ♮ of the second chord is continued through the third chord, as indicated by the line placed after the natural.

Ex. 89.

EXERCISES.

Harmonize the following, introducing the first inversion of the Mediant Triad at each of the places indicated:—

Harmonize the following basses in accordance with the figuring :—

CHAPTER XIII.

THE LEADING-NOTE TRIAD—FIRST INVERSION.

89. *In both Major and Minor keys*, the fifth from the Leading-note or seventh degree of the scale, being a diminished fifth, the triad which is formed upon this note is a Diminished Triad, thus :—

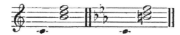

This triad is a discord and will be considered with the other dissonant triads in Chapter XVI.

90. **First Inversion.**—As in the first inversion of this triad, the dissonant interval (the augmented fourth or its inversion, the diminished fifth) occurs only between two of the upper parts. This inversion of the chord may be freely employed in both Major and Minor keys, thus :—

91. **Ear Exercises** (to be dictated also in C minor) :—

This chord is employed with the best effect when it is preceded or followed by the Tonic Triad or its first inversion, as shown above. Either the bass note or the third from the bass may be doubled, but not the sixth, which is the Leading-note. Provided the Leading-note rises, the progression of the chord is unrestricted.

92. **Harmonic Progression.**—The progression of a perfect fifth to a diminished fifth, as shown in Ex. 92 (*a*), as well as the reverse of this, the progression of a diminished fifth to a perfect fifth, as in (*b*), both of which may be formed between this chord and the Tonic Triad or its first inversion, are allowed (see par. 83). *Progressions formed of two diminished fifths*, such as may be formed in the Minor key between the first inversions of the triads upon the Supertonic and the Leading-note, as in (*c*), *are also allowed.*

Ex. 92.

93. **The Minor Seventh as a Melody Note in the Minor Key.**—When a melody in the Minor key takes the descending form of the Melodic Minor scale, and proceeds stepwise from the Tonic down to the Submediant by the employment of the minor seventh, this latter note is frequently harmonized by a chord of the sixth upon the Supertonic, the minor seventh taking the place of the major seventh or Leading-note, as in Ex. 93 (*a*). The minor seventh may also be harmonized by a chord of the sixth upon the Dominant, in which case it becomes the third from the bass, as in Ex. 93 (*b*), but this is a less familiar harmonization than the previous one.

Ear Exercises:—

Ex. 93.

EXERCISES.

Harmonize the following, introducing the first inversion of the Leading-note triad at each of the places indicated :—

In the following melodies the Minor Seventh is to be harmonized by a chord of the sixth either upon the Supertonic or upon the Dominant:—

Harmonize the following Basses in accordance with the figuring:—

CHAPTER XIV.

THE PRIMARY TRIADS IN THEIR SECOND INVERSION

94. The TONIC TRIAD—Second Inversion.—The second inversion of a triad has the fifth of the original chord in the bass. The second inversion of the Tonic Triad is shown in Ex. 94 (*b*).

The root and the third of the original chord have now become the fourth and the sixth from the bass respectively, and the figuring of the chord is $^6_4$. *In the second inversion of all consonant triads, the best note to double (with one exception) is the bass note*, that is, the fifth of the chord in its original position. It is possible, however, to double either of the other notes, provided such note be not the Leading-note.

95. Ear Exercises (also in C minor, except (*e*)):—

96 **The Progression of the Bass** WHEN APPROACHING AND QUITTING A SIX-FOUR CHORD :—The second inversion of a common chord, owing to the fact that one of its notes stands at the distance of a Perfect fourth from the bass, is always subject to special rules of progression. The interval of the Perfect fourth as an inversion of the Perfect fifth, is included amongst the perfect consonances, and when it is heard in a chord, between two of the upper parts, it produces no dissonant effect. When, however, it is heard as the fourth from the bass, it loses to some extent its perfectly consonant character and the chord of which it forms part is not allowed that free and unrestricted progression which belongs to the root position and first inversion of common chords. The rules to which the second inversion of common chords are subject, refer entirely to the progression of the bass part, both as to the approaching and the quitting of the bass note of the $\frac{6}{4}$ chord. They are as follows :—

I —When a $\frac{6}{4}$ chord is both *preceded* and *followed* by other positions of the same chord, the bass note of the $\frac{6}{4}$ chord may be approached and quitted by any interval, see Ex 95 (*a*).

II.—When a $\frac{6}{4}$ chord is *preceded* by another chord in its root position, the bass part is free to move to the bass note of the $\frac{6}{4}$ chord either by a step, as in (*b*), or by a leap, as in (*c*).

III.—When a $\frac{6}{4}$ chord is *preceded* by an inversion of another chord, the bass part must move to the bass note of the $\frac{6}{4}$ chord by a step, as in (*d*) and (*e*).

IV —A $\frac{6}{4}$ chord may be *preceded* or *followed* by a different chord (root position or inversion) upon the same bass note, see Ex. 99 (*a*).

V.—When a $\frac{6}{4}$ chord is *followed* by a different chord (that is, except when the same chord is repeated in another position, as in Ex. 95 (*a*)), the bass must either remain stationary, as in (*b*) and (*d*), leap an octave, as in (*c*), or move by the step of a second, either upwards or downwards, as in (*e*)

VI.—When a $\frac{6}{4}$ chord, which is preceded by a different chord, is *followed* by another position of the same chord, the bass part, when the harmony changes, should return to a note, to which a correct progression from the $\frac{6}{4}$ chord could have been made, as in (*f*).

97. **The "Cadential Six-four" Chord, and the "Imperfect Cadence."**—In examples (*b*), (*c*), and (*d*), given above, it will be seen that the second inversion of the Tonic Chord is employed immediately before the two chords which form the final cadence. In this position, *this* $\frac{6}{4}$ chord is both familiar and valuable. There is however another position which it frequently occupies, and in which it is hardly less familiar or less valuable, that is, as the first chord of one form of the "*Imperfect Cadence*" or "*half-close on the Dominant*," one of the MIDDLE CADENCES referred to in par 78 In the following example this chord is seen in both positions, at (*a*) forming part of a half close on the Dominant and at (*b*) as leading to a Perfect Cadence :—

Ex. 96.

When a ⁶₄ chord is employed in either of these positions it is called a "*cadential* ⁶₄." A "cadential ⁶₄" nearly always occurs upon a stronger beat of the bar, or upon a stronger portion of a beat, than the chord which immediately follows it, and as a general rule the sixth and the fourth of the first chord move respectively to the fifth and the third of the second chord. The single exception to this rule, as to the position of the cadential ⁶₄ chord, occurs when the ⁶₄ chord is both preceded and followed by chords upon the same bass note, as in Ex. 99 (*a*). In connection with the figuring of the above example, it should be noticed that *when a triad is preceded by a different chord upon the same bass note*, (as is the case in both the second and third bars above), *the triad requires to be figured*, otherwise it would be understood that the figuring of the first bass note applied also to the second bass note. Sometimes both chords are sounded over one sustained note, as shown below. The two sets of figures are then placed under this one note. In such cases, each chord either takes half the value of the note, as in (*c*), or in the case of a dotted note, the first chord takes two-thirds of the value, as in (*d*).

The employment of a ⁶₄ chord, not cadentially, but as a "*passing* ⁶₄" is shown in Ex. 95 (*e*), and when so employed it may be upon either an accented or an unaccented beat of the bar.

98. **Allowable Hidden Octaves.**—Hidden octaves which are formed between the outside parts when proceeding to the second inversion of a common chord, are allowed, provided either the bass moves a fourth and the highest part a second, as in Ex. 97 (*a*), or the bass moves a second and the highest part a fourth, as in (*b*) :—

Ex. 97.

EXERCISES.

Harmonize the following, introducing the second inversion of the Tonic Triad at each of the places indicated :—

₊ Some further exercises upon the employment of the second inversion of the Tonic Triad, used cadentially, will be found at the end of Chap. XVII on Cadences.

---

99. The DOMINANT TRIAD—Second Inversion.

Ear Exercises (also in C minor) :—

Ex. 98.

The second inversion of the Dominant Triad is used almost entirely as a "passing ⁶₄," either between repetitions of the Tonic Triad or between the Tonic Triad and its first inversion as shown above.

EXERCISES.

Harmonize the following, introducing the second inversion of the
Dominant Triad at each of the places indicated :—

100. The SUBDOMINANT TRIAD—Second Inversion.

Ear Exercises (also in C minor) :—

The second inversion of the Subdominant Triad is used chiefly
cadentially, as one of the forms of the Plagal Cadence in the manner
shown in (a).

101. **Consecutive Perfect Fourths with the Bass.**—
Now that it is possible to employ two ⁶₄ chords upon adjacent bass
notes (the second inversions of the Dominant and Subdominant Triads),
although such a progression would neither be a very familiar nor useful
one, yet the following rule must be brought to the pupil's notice. *In
any progression of ⁶₄ chords, no part may proceed in perfect fourths with
the bass.* When two ⁶₄ chords are employed upon adjacent bass notes,
as in Ex. 100, the fourths in the two chords, if they are both perfect
fourths, must not appear in the same part, as in (a) but in different
parts, as in (b).

EXERCISES.

Harmonize the following, introducing the second inversion of the Subdominant Triad at each of the places indicated :—

Harmonize the following, introducing the second inversion of one of the Primary Triads at each of the places indicated :—

CHAPTER XV.

THE SECONDARY TRIADS IN THEIR SECOND INVERSION.

102. The second inversions of the consonant Secondary Triads, are the second inversion of the Submediant Triad in both major and minor keys, see Ex. 101 (*a*), and the second inversions of the Supertonic and the Mediant Triads in the major key, see (*b*) and (*c*). Neither of these second inversions are very useful nor very familiar. They are rarely to be met with, and the occasions when the pupil will wish to use either of them in preference to any other chord will be few and far between. For the sake of completeness, however, it is necessary that they should be mentioned, and a few exercises upon them should be given. As in the following exercises, when they are employed it is generally as "passing $\frac{6}{4}$" chords, the bass moving in stepwise progression. In the second inversion of the Mediant Triad, the bass note, being the Leading-note, may not be doubled. With this exception the rule as to the doubling of notes, given in par. 94, applies also to these chords.

Ear Exercises:—

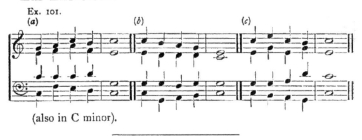

(also in C minor).

EXERCISES.

Harmonize the following, introducing the second inversion of a Triad at each of the places indicated :—

Harmonize the following basses in accordance with the figuring :—

CHAPTER XVI.

THE DISSONANT TRIADS.

103. We have now to consider those triads which on account of their dissonant character require special treatment. These comprise *the Diminished Triad upon the Leading-note* in both Major and Minor keys, as shown in Ex. 102 (*a*) and (*b*)), *the Diminished Triad upon the Supertonic in the Minor key*, as in (*c*), and *the Augmented Triad upon the Mediant in the Minor key*, as in (*d*), as well as *the second inversion of each of these triads.*

Ex. 102.

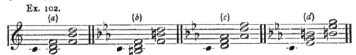

In each of these triads and their second inversion a dissonant interval is formed between the bass note and one of the other notes of the chord, and the notes which form this dissonant interval must proceed in such a manner that a satisfactory musical effect shall be left upon the mind of the listener, in other words, *the dissonant interval must be resolved.* The subject of Discords and their Resolution can only be touched upon quite incidentally in this chapter, but it will be more fully dealt with in connection with the chord of the Dominant Seventh (Chapter XIX).

104. **The LEADING-NOTE TRIAD** (DIMINISHED TRIAD).
Ear Exercises (also in C minor):—

Ex. 103.

In the original position of this triad, which is the same in both Major and Minor keys, the dissonant interval, the Diminished fifth from the bass, may either fall a second to the third of the Tonic chord, as in (*a*), or it may remain to be a note of the next chord, as in (*b*). The bass note always rises a step to the Tonic, unless the chord be repeated in another position. The third of the chord should be doubled. This triad is frequently regarded as an incomplete form of the chord of the

Dominant Seventh, of which it forms the three highest notes. When it is so described the root, of course, is the Dominant. *The second inversion* of this triad resolves upon the first inversion of the Tonic Triad, as in (*s*), and the progression of the two notes which form the dissonant interval (the Augmented fourth) is the same, as in (*a*), except that their relative position is now reversed. In neither of these forms is this chord often to be met with, and the pupil should rarely make use of it except in exercises where it is specially indicated.

105. **Consecutive Fifths and Consecutive Fourths with the Bass.**—*The progression of a Perfect fifth to a Diminished fifth, formed between the bass and an upper part,* as shown between the alto and bass parts of the first two chords in Ex. 103 (*a*), *is freely allowed,* but the reverse of this, a Diminished fifth followed by a Perfect fifth between the bass and an upper part is *not* allowed. In Ex. 103 (*c*), where the second inversion of this triad is preceded by the second inversion of the Tonic triad, the tenor part moves in fourths with the bass. It should, however, be noticed, that although the first fourth is a Perfect fourth, the second is an Augmented fourth. *The progression of a Perfect fourth to an Augmented fourth, formed between the bass and an upper part* (provided the parts move by step) *is freely allowed.* Such consecutive fourths will be frequently met with in connection with the last inversion of the chord of the Dominant seventh (Chapter XIX). The reverse of this progression, an Augmented fourth followed by a Perfect fourth, is not incorrect, but it is a far less familiar progression and in these early stages should be avoided.

EXERCISES.

Harmonize the following, introducing the Leading-note Triad or its second inversion at each of the places indicated :—

106. **The SUPERTONIC TRIAD in the MINOR KEY** (Diminished Triad).—Although this triad in the minor key, and also that upon the Mediant in the same key (par. 108), owing to the fact that they are both discords (and the progression of some of their notes therefore restricted), differ, in their nature from the corresponding triads in the major key, which are concords, yet, the function of each of these triads, in both major and minor keys, is not essentially different ; that is, allowing for the limitations of correct resolution and progression, the chords to which each can most effectively proceed are the same in both keys. This will be seen by a comparison of Ex. 80 (*d*) and Ex. 95 (*c*) with Ex. 104 (*a*) and (*b*) respectively, and in connection with the Mediant Triad, a comparison of the last two exercises in Ex. 86 with Ex. 106 (*a*)

and (*b*). In the resolution of both of these dissonant triads, it will be seen that the best progression is formed when the root of the next chord is a fourth above that of the discord, as in Ex. 104 (*a*) and Ex. 106 (*a*). Later on it will be seen that this is the most familiar progression of roots formed by discords and their resolution.

Ear Exercises:—

Ex. 104.

In the original position of this triad, the Diminished fifth from the bass is resolved either by falling a second, as in Ex. 104 (*a*) and (*b*), or by remaining stationary and becoming a note of the next chord, as in (*c*). The progression of the bass note is not restricted, and either this note or the third may be doubled. When this triad is preceded by the Tonic Triad in its root position, the fifth from the Tonic (a Perfect fifth) may proceed to the fifth of the Supertonic (a Diminished fifth), as at (*c*), (see par. 105). *In the second inversion*, the bass note (which was the Diminished fifth in the original chord) falls a second, as in (*d*). This inversion is rarely to be met with.

107. **The Major Sixth as a Melody Note in the Minor Key.**—When a melody in the Minor key takes the ascending form of the Melodic Minor scale, and proceeds stepwise from the Dominant to the Leading-note by the employment of the Major sixth, the Major sixth may be harmonized by a Minor Common Chord upon the Supertonic, as in Ex. 105 (*a*) and (*b*). When the Minor Common Chord on the Supertonic is so employed, it is generally followed by a chord of the sixth upon the same bass note, as in (*a*), but it may also be followed by a Dominant chord, as in (*b*). A chord of the sixth upon the Tonic is also sometimes employed to harmonize this note, as shown in (*c*).

Ear Exercises:—

Ex. 105.

The harmonization of this Major sixth in the Minor key by a Major triad upon the Subdominant, although occasionally to be met with in the works of old composers, is very rarely employed by modern composers.

EXERCISES.

Harmonize the following, introducing the Supertonic Triad or its second inversion at each of the places indicated :—

In the following, the Major sixth (*) is to be harmonized by a Minor Common Chord on the Supertonic :—

108. The MEDIANT TRIAD in the MINOR KEY (AUGMENTED TRIAD).

Ear Exercises :—

Ex. 106.

In the resolution of this triad *in its original position*, the bass nearly always rises a fourth (or falls a fifth) to the Submediant, and the chord resolves either upon the Submediant triad, as in (*a*), or the first inversion of the Subdominant triad, as in (*b*). The Augmented fifth is resolved by rising a semitone to the Tonic, and either the bass note or the third of the chord is doubled. *In the second inversion* this chord resolves upon a Tonic triad, as in (*c*), the sixth from the bass being doubled.

109. **Harmonic Progression.**—*The progression of an Augmented fifth to a Perfect fifth* (or *vice versa*), which may be formed in the Minor key between the triad upon the Mediant and one of the common chords of the key, or an inversion of such, as shown below, *is not allowed :—*

Bad.

EXERCISES.

Harmonize the following, introducing the Mediant Triad, or its second inversion, at each of the places indicated :—

Harmonize the following Basses in accordance with the figuring :—

IX.—Taking Ex. 103 as your model, construct two similar series of progressions in the keys of A major and F minor, illustrating the employment of the Leading-note triad and its second inversion.

X.—Taking Exs. 104 and 106 as your models, construct similar series of progressions in the keys of B minor and E flat minor, illustrating the employment of the triads upon the Supertonic and the Mediant, and their second inversions.

₊ Of the Triads mentioned in this chapter, those upon the Supertonic and Mediant in the Minor key, in their original position, are both useful and fairly familiar chords, but the Triad upon the Leading-note, and the second inversion of all three Triads, are rarely to be met with, and should be very rarely employed. They are mentioned merely for the sake of completeness.

CHAPTER XVII.

CADENCES.*

(ALSO THE CONSTRUCTION OF FOUR-BAR EXERCISES TO ILLUSTRATE THE EMPLOYMENT OF DIFFERENT FORMS OF CADENCE).

110. When a succession of chords is brought to a final termination in a musically satisfactory manner, or its progress is temporarily arrested, or we might say punctuated, (as in the second bar of the following example), a CADENCE is said to be formed thus :—

Ex. 107.

A Cadence means a close, and cadences mark the close or completion of such portions of a musical composition as phrases, sentences or sections, as well as the close of the entire composition. It naturally follows, therefore, that there are different varieties of cadence, which produce different degrees of finality in their musical effect, and cadences are described and classified according to the nature of this effect. The simplest form of classification is to divide cadences into two classes, namely :—I. FINAL CADENCES, or cadences which can be employed to terminate a composition ; and II. MIDDLE CADENCES, or cadences which can be employed only during the progress of a composition.

111. I. **Final Cadences.**—In these, the Tonic chord in its root position is always the second and final chord, and it is generally preceded either by the Dominant chord (triad or discord) or the Subdominant chord. When both the chords forming the cadence are in their root position, it is called a *Full Close* or a *Full Cadence*, thus :—

Ex. 108.

* Although some forms of Cadence have already been briefly referred to, yet, in order that the nature and classification of cadences may be considered with as much completeness as possible, in the present chapter, reference to such cadences will be included even at the cost of some small amount of repetition.

A Full Cadence which is formed by the progression of the Dominant chord to the Tonic chord, as Ex. 108 (*a*) or (*b*), is called an *Authentic* or *Perfect Cadence*, and one which is formed by the progression of the Subdominant chord to the Tonic chord, as (*c*), is called a *Plagal Cadence*. In Perfect cadences the effect of finality is most completely attained when the highest part is formed either by the Leading-note or the Supertonic proceeding to the Tonic, as in (*a*) and (*b*) respectively; while in Plagal cadences it is best to repeat the Tonic in the highest part, as in (*c*). The Plagal Cadence is found chiefly in old music and in church music generally, while the Authentic Cadence belongs specially to modern music, and represents the feeling for modern tonality.

112. **Inverted Cadences.**—If either or both of the chords of a Full Cadence be in an inverted form, an *Inverted Cadence* is formed. When only the first chord of the cadence is inverted, as in Ex. 109 (*a*) and (*b*), the cadence still remains a Final cadence; but should the final Tonic chord be inverted, as in (*c*), the cadence ceases to be a Final cadence and becomes a Middle cadence. Another form of inverted cadence is formed by the first inversion of the Leading-note triad as in (*d*).

Ex. 109.

In all the cadences in Ex. 108 and 109, it will be noticed that, with one exception, the second chord is upon a stronger beat of the bar than the first chord. This is generally the case in Final cadences. The exception shown in Ex. 109 (*b*) is due to the fact that both chords have the same bass note, and therefore the first one may be upon the stronger beat. Compare Ex. 99 (*a*).

113. II. **Middle Cadences.**—Middle Cadences may be subdivided into *Imperfect Cadences* (which are also called *Half Cadences* or *Half Closes*), and *Interrupted Cadences*.

IMPERFECT or HALF CADENCES have the Dominant Triad in its root position for their final chord, and it may be preceded by almost any other triad, or inversion of such. Some of the most useful forms are given below:—

Ex. 110.

In INTERRUPTED CADENCES the Dominant chord, instead of being followed by the Tonic chord, as in a Perfect Cadence, is followed by another chord, generally that upon the Submediant, and the effect of finality which would have been produced is interrupted, hence the name "Interrupted Cadence." Such cadences are also called *False* or *Deceptive Cadences.* Ex. 111 shows two forms of such cadences.

Ex. III.

For **Ear Exercises,** to test the pupil's power of discriminating the various cadences by their sound, the teacher should play different cadences for the pupil to name, after hearing the key-chord sounded beforehand.

EXERCISES.

I. Write examples of the following Cadences in the keys of B flat major and F sharp minor :—A Perfect cadence, a Plagal cadence, an Inverted Perfect cadence, and an Inverted Plagal cadence, all to be *Final cadences;* also the following *Middle cadences,* two different forms of the Interrupted cadence, six different forms of Half cadences, and an Inverted Middle cadence.

Harmonize the following, introducing some suitable form of cadence at each of the places indicated. Describe each cadence you employ :—

VI.—Taking Ex. 96 as your model, construct passages of four bars in length (consisting of triads and their inversions) in the keys of G, E flat, and B major, and D, C sharp, and F minor. Each passage must illustrate the employment of the second inversion of the Tonic Triad used cadentially in two different ways, (1) as forming an Imperfect Cadence in the second bar, and (2) as leading to a Final Cadence in the third bar (see Model worked below).

VII.—Taking Ex. 107 as your model, construct similar passages of four bars in length in the keys of F, A, and D flat major, and E, G, and F sharp minor. In these, the cadence in the second bar must be an Interrupted Cadence to the Submediant.

*** SUGGESTIONS AS TO THE CONSTRUCTION OF FOUR-BAR EXERCISES TO ILLUSTRATE THE EMPLOYMENT OF MIDDLE AND FINAL CADENCES.

FIRST STEP.—Write down in the key of the Exercise everything which is already determined, thus :—

Model in C minor for Ex. VI.

Either the higher or the lower G's may be taken, whichever, with the bass notes eventually to be added, will make the better bass part. This point should be left undecided until the *Fourth Step* is reached.

SECOND STEP.—Indicate suitable Treble notes over the chords which are already determined. In this matter there are several possible notes to be selected from. We have indicated some of the most obvious ones :—

THIRD STEP.—Construct a simple Treble part which will be suitable to lead from one fixed point to the next, thus :—

If the pupil is sufficiently musical to conceive both melody and harmony together, this step and the next one will practically merge into one mental operation, but if he is unable to do this, he must consciously proceed to the next step.

FOURTH STEP—Supply suitable harmonies to the above melody, and indicate such by means of a figured bass, thus :—

FINAL STEP.—Complete the Exercise by filling in the two middle parts.

[Ex. VII may be worked in an exactly similar manner. The only difference between Ex. VI and VII being in the nature of the Middle Cadence].

CHAPTER XVIII.

SEQUENCES.

114. When a melody or a progression of chords is repeated not less than twice, each repetition starting upon a different degree of the scale, but the whole series proceeding in some regular manner, either ascending or descending, a SEQUENCE is said to be formed, thus :—

Ex. 112.

Ex. 113.

A Sequence in which the repetitions of the original progression occur only in one part, the other parts present moving in an independent manner, as in Ex. 112, is called a MELODIC SEQUENCE; while one in which two or more parts move as in the original progression, as in Ex. 113, where all the four parts so move, is called a HARMONIC SEQUENCE. An examination of the above Sequences will show that the intervals and chords which correspond with one another in the original progression, and in the different repetitions, only agree with one another *numerically* and *not qualitatively*. Thus, the interval of a Perfect fourth which is formed between the first and second treble notes of the original progression in Ex. 113 is represented in the first repetition by an Augmented fourth, and in the second by a Diminished fourth, and only in the third by another Perfect fourth ; while the first chord, which in the original progression is a Minor triad, is represented in the first repetition by a Diminished triad, and in the second by an Augmented triad. Sequences of this kind are called *Tonal Sequences.*

115. **Exceptional Progression in Tonal Sequences** — In Tonal Sequences exceptional freedom of treatment and progression is allowed in the formation of the repetitions of the sequence. Thus,

provided there is no fault in the original progression or text of the sequence, and also that no faulty progression occurs between the last chord of this initial progression and the first chord of the first repetition, then, no account need be taken of faulty Melodic or Harmonic progressions which may be formed by the parts forming the repetitions of the sequence. It may be helpful to the pupil, if we indicate the directions in which, under these special circumstances, the ordinary rules of progression are relaxed. In the repetitions of a Sequence—

(1) An Augmented interval may occur in any part ;

(2) The Leading-note may be doubled, and it may either rise or fall ;

(3) Dissonant triads may be employed with the same freedom as Common chords, that is, the dissonant note may be doubled and its progression is unrestricted.

The pupil will now understand that all of the apparently incorrect progressions in Ex. 113 are justified by their occurring in one of the repetitions of a sequence.

116. **Real Sequences.**—Besides Tonal sequences, in which, as we stated above, the repetitions are not the real counterparts of the original progression, there are sequences of another kind, in which the several intervals and chords of the various repetitions do exactly correspond qualitatively as well as numerically with those of the original progression. Such are called *Real Sequences,* and the following is an example of this kind of sequence :—

Ex. 114.   etc.

As will be seen from this example, Real Sequences generally involve modulation to extreme keys. Their formation is quite simple but they are rarely employed for many repetitions.

<hr>

EXERCISES.

Harmonize the following Basses in accordance with the figuring. Where the bass part progresses sequentially, the upper parts should also move sequentially :—

CHAPTER XIX.

THE CHORD OF THE DOMINANT SEVENTH.

117. The chords which come next to the Triads in simplicity of construction are those of the seventh. A chord of the seventh is formed by adding to a triad a note which is a seventh from the root of the triad, thus :—

Ex. 115.

118. A chord of the seventh may be formed upon every note of the diatonic scale, but the most important as well as the most familiar and useful chord of the seventh is that which is formed upon the Dominant, and is called the CHORD OF THE DOMINANT SEVENTH, thus :—

Ex. 116.

The notes of this chord are exactly the same in both a Major key and its Tonic Minor key, and the intervals of which it is composed are, a Major third, a Perfect fifth, and a Minor seventh, reckoning, of course, from the root. The interval of the seventh being a dissonant interval, the chord of the Dominant seventh and all chords of the sevenths are what are called "*discords*."

119. **Discords, their Nature and Resolution.** — The term "discord," as employed in music, has not the same meaning as when it is employed in connection with non-musical matters. Musical discords are not only neither necessarily disagreeable nor unpleasant, but in the majority of instances are distinctly agreeable and pleasant. It is no exaggeration to say, that most of the charm which music possesses is due to the skilful employment of discords. When applied to a chord in music, the term "discord" simply means that *the effect of such a chord is to leave the listener, musically speaking, unsatisfied.* If the above chords be sounded, one cannot fail to recognize their unsatisfying nature, while if either chord be repeated several times, it seems to become more unsatisfying after each repetition. The fact is, that EVERY DISCORD REQUIRES TO BE FOLLOWED BY SOME OTHER CHORD, WHICH SHALL SUPPLY THAT FEELING OF MUSICAL SATISFACTION OR REST, FOR WHICH THE DISCORD HAS CREATED THE DESIRE, and this feeling of satisfaction is only completely produced when the notes which form the dissonant interval move in some special

manner to certain of the notes of the next chord, thus effecting what is called THE RESOLUTION OF THE DISCORD.

120. **The Resolution of the Dominant Seventh.**—In the chord of the Dominant seventh, the notes whose progression is restricted so that a satisfactory resolution of the discord may be obtained are the third and the seventh, which between them form either a Diminished fifth or its inversion, an Augmented fourth, according to their relative position.   As will be seen from the following Ear Exercises, *the seventh must either fall a second*, as in Ex. 117 (*a*) and (*b*), *or remain stationary*, as in (*c*), *while the third, the Leading-note of the key, must always rise a second to the Tonic.*

EAR EXERCISES (Root Position):—

Ex. 117.

** All the above, except (*d*), should be dictated also in C minor. In doing so, it should not be forgotten, that in the chord of the seventh, as in the Dominant triad, the B's are "natural" (not flat).

The most familiar resolution of the chord of the Dominant seventh is *upon the Tonic Triad in its root position*, as shown in (*a*).   The seventh of the Dominant chord then falls to the third of the Tonic chord, and the third of the Dominant chord rises to the root of the Tonic chord. In this resolution the fifth of the Tonic chord is generally omitted. The chord of the Dominant seventh followed by the Tonic Triad in this manner absolutely defines the key of a passage, and is the most familiar form of the Perfect Cadence, see (*e*)†.   Another familiar resolution is *upon the Submediant Triad in its root position*, as shown in (*b*).   Here, the seventh and the third proceed as in the previous resolution, but to the fifth and the third of the Submediant Triad, respectively.   This resolution is often employed to form an Interrupted Cadence, as in (*e*)*. A less familiar resolution is *upon the first inversion of the Subdominant Triad*, as shown in (*c*), where the seventh remains stationary to become a note of the next chord.   The seventh occasionally moves to another note of the chord before proceeding to its proper resolution, as shown in (*f*). A resolution of this kind is called an "ornamental resolution." The progression of the fifth of the Dominant chord is unrestricted, and if desired, it may be omitted, as in the first chord of Ex. 119. In such cases the root is doubled, and it is the only note which may be doubled. It is possible to omit the third of the chord—the root, fifth and seventh only being present—but this is rarely done.*

121. Harmonic Progression.—In the resolution of this chord, such progressions as the following, where the intervals of the seventh and ninth proceed by similar motion to an octave, as in Ex. 118 (*a*) and (*b*) respectively, and where the interval of a second proceeds similarly to a unison, as in (*c*), are strictly forbidden :—

Ex. 118.

(*a*) and (*b*) illustrate "hidden octaves" in a form, which, whether between outside or inner parts, is equally bad. These, and all similar progressions which it may be possible to form in connection with chords to be studied later on, infringe the following important rule of harmonic progression :—

No two notes next to one another in alphabetical order, and being sounded together, may proceed by similar motion to an octave or a unison.

122. The Repetition of a Discord.—The chord of the Dominant seventh (or any other discord) may be repeated any number of times before proceeding to its resolution, this being delayed until after the final repetition, as in Ex 119. When a discord is repeated in this manner, the dissonant note or notes may be transferred from one part to any other part, their resolution eventually taking place in those parts in which they last appear, thus :—

Ex. 119.

The Augmented fourth formed in the treble part between the third and fourth chords, is not incorrect, as both notes belong to the same chord (see par. 47).

---

* The chromatic resolutions of the chord of the Dominant seventh will be explained in Part II, in connection with the chromatic chords upon which such resolutions are made.

123. **The Figuring of the Chord of the Dominant Seventh.**—The complete figuring of this chord would naturally be $\frac{7}{5}$, but unless either the fifth or the third require modification by means of an accidental, this is abbreviated to the single figure, 7. In the figuring in the Minor key, the third of the chord being the Leading-note, the employment of an accidental to indicate the inflection required by this note is always necessary. The figuring in the keys of C major and of C minor would therefore be as follows :—

Ex. 120.

EXERCISES.

I. Regard each of the following notes as the third of a Dominant chord, prefix the correct key-signature of the major key, and place under each, the chord of the Dominant Seventh, resolving it (*a*) upon the Tonic Triad, (*b*) upon the Submediant Triad and (*c*) upon the first inversion of the Subdominant Triad :—

II. Regard each of the above notes as the seventh of a Dominant chord, prefix the correct key-signature of the major key, and place under each the chord of the Dominant Seventh, resolving it in the three ways mentioned in Ex. I.

III. Regard each of the following notes as the fifth of a Dominant chord, prefix the correct key-signature of the minor key, and place under each the chord of the Dominant Seventh, resolving it in the three ways mentioned in Ex. I :—

Harmonize the following, introducing a chord of the Dominant Seventh at each of the places indicated, and correctly resolving it upon the next chord :—

FIRST INVERSION.

124. The chord of the Dominant Seventh, when inverted, may have either the third, the fifth, or the seventh of the original chord as the bass note, and it has therefore three inversions. *In* ALL *of these inversions however, with one exception (to be mentioned in connection with the Second Inversion), the progression of the notes which were the third and the seventh in the original chord, is the same as when they appeared in the chord in its Root position.*

125. The FIRST INVERSION has the third of the original chord for its bass note, thus :—

Ex. 121.

The fifth, the seventh, and the root of the original chord are now respectively a third, a fifth, and a sixth from the new bass note, which is the Leading-note of the key. The complete figuring of the first inversion would be $\frac{6}{5}$, but it is abbreviated to $\frac{6}{5}$, as shown above, unless the third requires modification by means of an accidental.

126. **Ear Exercises** (also in C minor) :—

Ex. 122.
(a)   (b)   (c)

*** The pupil should learn to discriminate between the different positions of the chord of the Dominant Seventh by their sound. With this object in view, the third progression in Ex. 117 (a) should be contrasted *in sound* with the second in Ex. 122 (a). In this first inversion, the bass note, the Leading-note, always rises a semitone to the Tonic, and that should help the pupil to recognize this position of the chord *by its sound.*

The resolution of this inversion *upon the Tonic Triad in its root position,* as shown in (*a*), is by far the most familiar and useful resolution. The resolutions *upon the first inversion of the Submediant Triad,* as shown in (*b*), and *upon the second inversion of the Subdominant Triad,* as shown in (*c*), are very much rarer than the corresponding resolutions of this discord in its root position.

EXERCISES.

VIII Regard each of the following notes as the seventh of a Dominant chord, prefix the correct key-signature of the major key and place under each the first inversion of the chord of the Dominant Seventh, resolving it (*a*) upon the Tonic Triad, (*b*) upon the first inversion of the Submediant Triad, and (*c*) upon the second inversion of the Subdominant Triad. In the two latter resolutions take as models for your exercises, Ex. 122 (*b*) and (*c*) :—

IX. Regard each of the last four notes of the above Exercise as the root of a Dominant chord, prefix the correct key-signature of the minor key, and place under each the first inversion of a chord of the Dominant Seventh, resolving it in the three above mentioned ways. Take Ex. 122 (*b*) and (*c*) as your models also in this exercise.

Harmonize the following, introducing the chord of the Dominant Seventh or its first inversion (whichever is suitable) at each of the places indicated :—

Harmonize the following, introducing the first inversion of the chord of the Dominant Seventh at each of the places indicated :—

SECOND INVERSION.

127. This inversion has the fifth of the original chord for its bass
note, thus :—

Ex. 123.

The seventh of the original chord is now a third, the root a fourth, and
the third a sixth from the bass note, which is the Supertonic of the key.
The complete figuring of this inversion would be $\frac{6}{4}$, but it is abbreviated
to $\frac{4}{3}$ unless, as in the Minor key, the sixth requires to be modified by an
accidental.   The full figuring is then necessary.

128. Ear Exercises (also in C minor) :—

Ex. 124.

₊ Contrast this inversion, *in sound*, both with the root position and
first inversion.

This inversion rarely resolves upon any other chord than that of the
Tonic, but it may resolve *upon the Tonic chord either in its root position,*
as shown above, *or in its first inversion,* as shown in Ex. 125.

129. Exceptional Progression of the Seventh.—When
this inversion resolves upon the first inversion of the Tonic chord, the
seventh falling a second, as in Ex. 125 (*a*), the third of the Tonic chord
(the bass note of its first inversion) is inevitably doubled.   Under these
circumstances, although in the Major key this is not desirable, it is
allowed.   In order, however, to avoid doubling the third of the Tonic
chord, *when the bass of the second inversion of the chord of the Dominant
seventh rises a second to the third of the Tonic chord, the seventh may also
rise a second to the fifth of the Tonic chord,* as in (*b*).   In this form of
resolution, when the root and the seventh are situated as adjacent
notes, that is, at the interval of a second apart, as in (*c*) and (*d*), they
must not proceed by oblique motion to an unison, as in (*d*), but the
root of the Dominant chord must leap to the root of the Tonic chord,
as in (*c*), (see par. 166).

Ear Exercises (also in C minor) :—

Ex. 125.

Bad.

EXERCISES.

XIV. Regard each of the following notes as the seventh of a Dominant chord, prefix the correct key-signature of the major key, and place under each the second inversion of the chord of the Dominant Seventh, resolving it (*a*) upon the Tonic Triad in its root position and (*b*) upon the Tonic Triad in its first inversion, the seventh resolving *upwards* :—

XV. Regard each of the above notes as the root of a Dominant chord, prefix the correct key-signature of the minor key, and place under each the second inversion of the chord of the Dominant Seventh, resolving it in the two above mentioned ways.

Harmonize the following, introducing the chord of the Dominant Seventh, either in its root position, or in its first, or second inversion (whichever is suitable), at each of the places indicated :—

Harmonize the following, introducing the second inversion of the chord of the Dominant Seventh at each of the places indicated :—

THIRD AND LAST INVERSION.

130. This inversion has the seventh of the original chord for its bass note, thus :—

Ex. 126.

The root of the chord is now a second from the bass, and the third and fifth of the original chord are now respectively a fourth and a sixth from the bass note, which is the Subdominant of the key. The complete figuring would be $\frac{6}{4}$, but this is abbreviated to $\frac{4}{2}$. In the Minor key the 4 always requires some form of modification, as illustrated above.

Ear Exercises (also in C minor) :—

Ex. 127.

⁎ Contrast this inversion, *in sound*, with the root position, and the first and second inversions.

As the seventh of the original chord, which is now in the bass, must fall a second, this inversion almost invariably resolves *upon the first inversion of the Tonic chord*. When the bass note of this inversion is approached by leap, it is better if the leap be made in an upward direction, as in (*b*), than in a downward one. The progression of fourths with the bass, in (*c*), the first fourth being a Perfect fourth, and the second, an Augmented fourth, is perfectly correct (see par. 105).

131. **The Interval of the Minor Seventh in Melody.**— Now that the interval of the Minor seventh may be formed by two notes belonging to the same chord (the chord of the Dominant seventh), it is possible to make use of it in a melody or part, at the same time it is not an interval which should be frequently employed for melodic purposes. When it is used in the bass part, it is less usual for both notes forming the interval to be harmonized by the chord of the Dominant seventh, than for the first note to be harmonized either by the Dominant Triad, as in Ex. 128 (*a*), or by the second inversion of the Tonic Triad, as in (*b*), and the second note by the last inversion of the Dominant seventh. The progression of the bass in (*b*), is not an infringement of the rules referring to the progression of the bass part when quitting a $\frac{6}{4}$ chord (par. 96), as F, in one sense, is *next* to G.

Ear Exercises (also in C minor) :—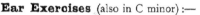

Ex. 128.

EXERCISES.

XX. Regard each of the following notes as the seventh of a Dominant chord, prefix the correct key-signature of the major key, and place over each the last inversion of the chord of the Dominant Seventh, resolving it upon the first inversion of the Tonic Triad :—

XXI. Regard each of the following notes as the third of a Dominant chord, prefix the correct key-signature of the minor key, and place under each the last inversion of the chord of the Dominant Seventh, resolving it upon the first inversion of the Tonic Triad :—

Harmonize the following, introducing the last inversion of the chord of the Dominant Seventh at each of the places indicated :—

Harmonize the following, introducing the chord of the Dominant Seventh and *all* its inversions in each exercise :—

₊ In working these Exercises, the pupil should decide, first of all, where he can introduce the different positions of the chord of the Dominant Seventh, followed by correct resolutions, and indicate these chords by figures under the bass part, which bass he must insert himself in connection with the melodies. After he has done this he should proceed in the usual way to harmonize the whole exercise.

Harmonize the following in accordance with the figures :—

XXX. Taking Ex. 117 (e) as your model, construct passages of
four bars in length in the keys of F, D, and A flat major, and E, G,
and C sharp minor, introducing the chord of the Dominant Seventh,
and some of its inversions, in each exercise.

CHAPTER XX.

NATURAL MODULATION.

132. MODULATION is the process of passing from one key to another. The first four chords in Ex. 129 illustrate a modulation from the key of C to the key of G, which is effected by means of the chord of the Dominant Seventh in the key of G,* (the key *to which* the modulation is made), resolving upon the Tonic triad in that key. Similarly, the last three chords illustrate another modulation, this time from the key of G back to the key of C, which is effected by cne chord of the Dominant Seventh in the key of C,† (the key *to which* the modulation is made), resolving upon the Tonic triad in that key.

Ex. 129.

Modulations are very frequently effected in the above manner, that is, by taking the chord of the Dominant Seventh (or an inversion of it) in the key *to which* the modulation is to be made, and resolving it upon the Tonic triad (or an inversion of it) in this new key

133. A modulation, or change of key, only takes place when there are at least *two* chords, which definitely leave one key and proceed to another. Thus, in Ex. 129, the third and fourth chords, *taken together*, belong to the key of G major, and cannot belong to any other key, but *either taken singly* could be employed in other keys and therefore would not define the key of G major. The same may be said with reference to the fifth and sixth chords, as representing the key of C major. Taken together, they effectually define this key, but taken singly they cannot do so. Modulations in which the new key prevails for only two or three chords, as in the above example, are sometimes called *Transitions* or *Transitory Modulations*. When a new key is definitely established in the mind of the listener, by the two chords which effect the modulation being immediately followed by other chords, characteristic of the new key, the modulation is sometimes described as *permanent*. In the following paragraphs, however, every change of key, whether of two or more chords, will be described simply as "a modulation."

134. Natural Modulation and Extraneous Modulation.—To every key there are certain other keys, which, because of their nearness in tonality, and the relationship which exists between their respective key-notes, are called *related (or attendant) keys.* The related keys to any major key are, the major keys of the Dominant and Subdominant, its own relative minor key, and the relative minor keys of the Dominant and Subdominant. The following shows the keys related to C major :—

F major.	**C major.**	G major.
D minor.	A minor.	E minor

The related keys to any minor key are, the minor keys of the Dominant and Subdominant, its own relative major key, and the relative major keys of the Dominant and Subdominant. The following shows the keys related to A minor, and it will be seen that they correspond with those given above as related to C major, the relative major of A minor :—

D minor.	**A minor.**	E minor.
F major.	C major.	G major.

It should be noted that the keys of C major and C minor, are *not*, in this sense, related keys. When a modulation is made from a key to one of its *related* keys it is called a NATURAL MODULATION, and when it is made to an *unrelated* key it is called an EXTRANEOUS MODULATION. The present chapter treats only of Natural Modulation, the subject of Extraneous Modulation being reserved for a later one (see Part II).

135. The "Connecting Link" in a Modulation.—In every modulation there is present some "connecting link" which forms a bond of union between the key *from which* the modulation is made, and that *to which* the modulation is made. *This link may take the form of a complete chord which can be employed in either key,* as in Ex. 130 (*a*), where the second chord could be the first inversion of either the Supertonic triad in C or of the Subdominant triad in A minor, *or the link may be merely a single note which is common to the two chords representing both keys,* as in Ex. 130 (*b*), where the note E is common both to the chord of C, and to the first inversion of the chord of the Dominant Seventh in A minor.

Ex. 130.

136. The Triad as the Connecting Link.—The following table of triads in C major and its related keys, will show the pupil, at a glance, the chords which are common to the different keys in any set of related keys, and which may be employed as connecting links in modulation between these keys. The various triads in the related keys are placed below the triad upon the corresponding bass note in the original key, and those triads which are identical with that in the original key are written entirely in semibreves, while, in those which differ, the particular notes which differ are written in black notes.

TABLE FOR COMPARING THE TRIADS IN A SET OF RELATED KEYS.

Ex. 131.

The above table will show that there are four triads in common between the keys of C and G, C and F, and C and A minor, three triads between C and E minor and one between C and D minor. Every major key has then at least one diatonic triad, which is common to that key and to any key which is related to it, and it is always possible therefore, when modulating to a related key, to employ a chord as the connecting link between the two keys. Most related keys, however, have several of such chords in common, and when modulating between these keys, it is possible, by the employment of the chords which are common to both keys, and the avoidance of those chords which belong only to one key, to, as it were, gradually "lean" towards the new key, and thereby effect a modulation with greater smoothness, than would otherwise be the case. Thus, in the following example, it would have been possible to have modulated from C major to A minor by the employment of the first chord and the last two chords only, this would have been what is sometimes described as a *Sudden* or *Direct Modulation*, but the abruptness of such a progression has been avoided by placing between the chord of C and the Dominant Seventh in A minor four other chords, all of which might belong either to the key of C major or that of A minor. In this example they belong to the key of C major, because a key prevails until a chord appears which effects a modulation from that key, and as the first chord which definitely modulates out of C is the chord of the Dominant Seventh upon E, only this chord and the last one are in A minor, all the previous being in C major. A modulation which is gradually led up to by chords common to both keys, is sometimes called a *Gradual Modulation*.

Ex. 132.

C major or A minor.

137. **The Tonic Triad as a Connecting Link.**—Referring once more to Ex. 131, and taking an individual triad, we find that the major common chord of C belongs not only to the key of C major, in which it is the Tonic chord, but also to the keys of G major, E minor, and F major, in which keys it is respectively the Subdominant, the Submediant, and the Dominant triad. When modulating from the key of C major to any of these keys, we may therefore always regard the major common chord on C as representing either key, and immediately follow it by some characteristic chord of the new key, such as the chord of the Dominant Seventh. This has been done in many of the Ear Exercises given to illustrate the manner of modulating to these keys, in which, in order to economise space, the Tonic triad in C is taken, *by itself*, as representing the key of C, and as the starting point of modulations to different keys (see par. 142 ***). When modulating to the keys of A minor and D minor, although the major common chord of C cannot be employed as a diatonic chord in either of these keys, yet its note E being also a note of the Dominant chord in each of these keys, forms a connecting link, and enables either of these chords to follow immediately after the triad of C, as in the Ear Exercises given to illustrate these modulations.

EXERCISE.—*The pupil should construct for himself a similar table to the above,* Ex. 131, *but in connection with the key of C minor and its related keys.* When he has done so, he will find that there are fewer chords which are common to a minor key and its related keys, than to a major key and its related keys, but that every key has one chord in common with each of its related keys.

138. **The Six-four Chord as a Connecting Link.**—The familiarity of the progression of the second inversion of a Tonic triad, followed immediately by the chord of the Dominant Seventh upon the same bass note, and leading to a Full Cadence, makes the second inversion of many triads, particularly useful chords for employing as connecting links, leading to modulations to keys of which the root of the second inversion is the Tonic, as shown in Ex. 133 :—

Ex. 133.

139. False Relation.—In the construction of modulations, it frequently happens that two chords are present, situated either next to one another, or with only one chord between, in which the same note (alphabetically) is employed, but inflected differently in each chord, as, for instance, the B natural and B flat in Ex. 134 (*a*). In such cases, the note which is so inflected should, if possible, be kept in the same part in both chords, as in (*b*), otherwise what is called a FALSE RELATION is produced. When the altered note has been correctly introduced, as in (*b*), it may then appear in any other part immediately afterwards, as at ✳, without creating any bad effect.

Ex. 134.

Bad. Good.

The employment of notes standing in false relation to one another does not always produce a bad musical effect, and it is therefore only in those special circumstances in which a bad effect is produced, that false relation is regarded as a fault. *The worst form of false relation (and the only form which is universally condemned) is that which is produced between two notes belonging to Common Chords or inversions of Common Chords, derived from the same root,* as illustrated in Ex. 134 (*a*). *This kind of false relation is strictly forbidden.*

It may help the pupil to understand the full significance of this rule, if we supplement it by examples of false relation which are allowed.

FALSE RELATION IS ALLOWED—

(1) Between the notes of two Common Chords, (or inversions of such), when the third of the first chord is either the root or the fifth of the second, as in Ex. 135 (*a*) and (*b*), respectively.

(2) Between the notes of a Common Chord, (or an inversion of such), and the first inversion of a Diminished triad, as in (*c*).

(3) Between the notes of a Common Chord, (or an inversion of such), and a Dominant discord (or other Fundamental discord, see Part II), as in (*d*).

(4) Between the minor seventh of the key, in the Minor key, and the third of the Dominant chord, when there is one chord between, as in (*e*).

Ex. 135.

Although none of the above are incorrect, yet a smoother progression would have been produced, both in (*a*) and (*b*), by keeping the inflected note in the same part, as shown below :—

Ex. 135.

140. **The Doubling of Notes.**—In passages which modulate, the rules which regulate the doubling of notes apply to the several notes of a chord, *regarded in that key to which it belongs at any particular moment*. Thus, in the second chord of Ex. 140, the Bass note being the Dominant of E minor, and *not* the Leading-note of C, the doubling of it is perfectly correct.

141. **Form of Ear Exercises.**—Each of the Ear Exercises which are given in connection with the different modulations, illustrate two different modulations. Thus, in the first series, which are given as illustrations of modulations to the key of the Dominant, assuming that the Tonic chord in C represents the key of C, there is first a modulation from the key of C to the key of G, the Dominant, and then a modulation from the key of G back to the key of C. This latter modulation, regarding G for the moment as the Tonic, is a modulation to the Subdominant of G. In the second series of Ear Exercises, which are given as illustrations of modulations to the key of the Subdominant, the reverse takes place, that is, the first modulation is from the key of C to that of F, the Subdominant, while the second is from the key of F back to that of C, which, regarding F for the moment as the Tonic, is a modulation to the Dominant of F. All the Ear Exercises in this chapter, which now follow, are constructed upon a similar plan, that is, each one illustrates two different modulations, *first*, a modulation from the key of C to one of its related keys, and, *secondly*, a modulation (which we call a complementary one), which returns from this related key back to the original key of C.

142. Modulation to the key of the Dominant (*by means of the chord of the Dominant Seventh and its inversions*) *with complementary return to the original key.*

Ear Exercises (*b*) to (*c*) also in C minor :—

*** BEFORE DICTATING EITHER OF THE EAR EXERCISES GIVEN UPON MODULATIONS, THE TEACHER SHOULD INVARIABLY ESTABLISH IN THE MIND OF THE PUPIL THE KEY OF C IN A MORE COMPLETE MANNER THAN IS DONE IN THE EAR EXERCISES, WHICH ARE MADE AS SHORT AS POSSIBLE, AND MERELY ILLUSTRATE THE ESSENTIAL POINTS OF THE MODULATION. THE PLAYING OF A FULL CADENCE CONSISTING OF THE CHORD OF THE DOMINANT SEVENTH RESOLVING UPON THE TONIC CHORD WOULD BE SUFFICIENT.

Ex. 136.

EXERCISE.—Taking the above as your models, construct four complete series of modulations to the key of the Dominant, by means of the chord of the Dominant Seventh and its inversions, starting from, and returning to, the keys of G and A flat major, and F and D sharp minor. In the major keys, the modulations should be made to the major key of the Dominant, and in the minor keys to the minor key of the Dominant, as shown in (*a*) and (*f*) respectively.

*** In this, and in all similar exercises in connection with other modulations, the employment of the root position and *every* inversion of the chord of the Dominant seventh should be illustrated in separate exercises.

Harmonize the following, modulating to the key of the Dominant at the places marked ⌐⌐⌐ , and returning to the original key immediately afterwards. A chord of the Dominant Seventh, or one of its inversions, should be employed both in modulating to the Dominant key and also in returning to the original key, as in the above Ear Exercises. In figuring the following after they have been harmonized, it should not be forgotten that *all* chords in which accidentals are employed, require those accidentals to be fully indicated in the figuring.

143. Modulation to the key of the Subdominant, *with complementary return to the original key.*

Ear Exercises:—

Ex. 137.

EXERCISE.—Taking the above as your models, construct two complete series of modulations to the key of the Subdominant, employing the chord of the Dominant Seventh and *all* its inversions, starting from, and returning to, the keys of A major and B flat minor.

Harmonize the following, modulating to the key of the Subdominant at the places marked and returning to the original key immediately afterwards :—

Harmonize the following, modulating to the keys of the Dominant and Subdominant, respectively, at the places indicated :—

*** It will be noticed in these Exercises, that the modulation to the key of the Dominant always comes *before* that to the Subdominant. In passages which modulate to both of these keys, this is the order in which these two modulations generally occur.

144. **Modulation from a Major key to the key of the Relative Minor,** *with complementary return to the original key (that is, a modulation from a Minor key to the key of the Relative Major).*

Ear Exercises :—

Ex. 138.

H

EXERCISE.—Taking the above (Ex. 138) as your models, construct two series of modulations to the key of the Relative Minor, employing the chord of the Dominant Seventh and *all* its inversions, starting from, and returning to, the keys of B flat and E major.

Harmonize the following, modulating to the key of the Relative Minor at each of the places indicated :—

145. **Modulation from a Minor key to the key of the Relative Major,** *with complementary return to the original key.*

Ear Exercises:—

EXERCISE.—Taking the above as your models, construct two series of modulations to the key of the Relative Major, employing the chord of the Dominant Seventh and *all* its inversions, starting from, and returning to, the keys of G minor and C sharp minor.

Harmonize the following, modulating to the key of the Relative Major at each of the places indicated :—

Harmonize the following, making a suitable modulation at each of the places indicated. It should be noticed that after a modulation, the new key is sometimes employed for one or more bars, and also that when the line is extended thus, ⌐⊤⌐, it should be followed by a modulation to another related key :—

146. **Modulation from a Major key to the Relative Minor key of the Dominant,** *with complementary return to the original key (that is, a modulation from a Minor key to the Relative Major of the Subdominant).*

Ear Exercises:—

Ex. 140.

EXERCISE —Taking the above as your models, construct two series of modulations to the Relative Minor key of the Dominant, starting from, and returning to, the keys of E flat and B major.

Harmonize the following, modulating to the Relative Minor key of the Dominant at each of the places indicated:—

147. **Modulation from a Minor key to the Relative Major of the Subdominant,** *with complementary return to the original key.*

Ear Exercises:—

Ex. 141.

EXERCISE.—Taking the above (Ex. 141) as your models, construct modulations to the Relative Major key of the Subdominant, starting from, and returning to, the keys of E minor and F minor.

Harmonize the following, modulating to the Relative Major key of the Subdominant at each of the places indicated :—

Harmonize the following, making a suitable modulation at each of the places indicated :—

148. **Modulation from a Major key to the Relative Minor of the Subdominant**, *with complementary return to the original key, (that is, a modulation from a Minor key to the Relative Major of the Dominant).*

Ear Exercises:—

Ex. 142.

EXERCISE.—Taking the above as your models, construct modulations to the Relative Minor key of the Subdominant, starting from, and returning to, the keys of A flat and F sharp major.

Harmonize the following, modulating to the Relative Minor key of the Subdominant at each of the places indicated :—

XXXIII.

XXXIV.

149. **Modulation from a Minor key to the Relative Major of the Dominant,** *with complementary return to the original key.*

Ear Exercises :—

Ex. 143.

EXERCISE.—Taking the above as your models, construct modulations to the Relative Major key of the Dominant, starting from, and returning to, the keys of D minor and G sharp minor.

Harmonize the following, modulating to the Relative Major key of the Dominant at each of the places indicated :—

XXXV.

XXXVI.

Harmonize the following, making a suitable modulation at each of the places indicated :—

XXXVII.

XXXVIII.

XLI.—Taking Exercises XIII to XVI as your models, construct passages of eight bars in length, in the keys of A and E flat major, and B and F minor, illustrating the employment of a half cadence in the second bar, a modulation to the Dominant at the fourth bar, and to the Subdominant at the fifth or sixth bar.

⁎ In this and the two following exercises, the pupil may proceed upon very similar lines to those suggested in connection with four-bar passages in Chap. XVII, starting thus :—

It is not improbable that several of the suggested chords will be employed in a different position or inversion to that which is selected, but the root progression at the places where the modulations are made, will not differ much from what is here shown.

XLII.—Construct passages of eight bars in length, in tne keys of B flat and E major, with similar modulations to the above, except the modulation at the fourth bar, which should be to the Relative Minor instead of to the Dominant.

XLIII.—Construct passages of eight bars in length, in the keys of D and C sharp minor, with similar modulations to the above, except the modulation at the fourth bar, which should be to the Relative Major instead of to the Dominant

CHAPTER XXI.

THE DIATONIC (OR SECONDARY) CHORDS OF THE SEVENTH.

150. In addition to the chord of the seventh upon the Dominant, a chord of the seventh, formed of the diatonic notes of the scale, may be employed upon any other degree of the major or minor scales.

Ex. 144.

An examination of the nature of these different chords, will show that they differ considerably with regard to the quality of the intervals of which they are composed, and not one of them, in this respect, corresponds exactly with the chord of the Dominant seventh.

151. In former times, when these chords were employed, they were subject to very strict treatment. It was necessary that the seventh should be *prepared*, by being present as a concord in the previous chord and in the same part, and that it should be *resolved* by falling a second to the third of a chord whose root was a fourth above, or a fifth below, that of the discord, thus :—

Ex. 145.

These restrictions have never had universal acceptance and are practically disregarded by modern composers. As, however, in some of the more dissonant forms of these chords, such preparation and resolution greatly add to the smoothness of the musical effect which is produced, in the present chapter, the above chords will be treated in the strict manner, and in the Exercises which follow, they must *always* be prepared and resolved according to the above mentioned conditions. It must be borne in mind, that the special treatment of the seventh, when it is employed in connection with the Leading-note Triad in both Major and Minor keys, and the Supertonic and Mediant Triads in the Minor key, in no way interferes with the special treatment required by other dissonant notes of the same chord (see Chap. XVI).

152. **Ear Exercises.**—The most useful of these chords of the
seventh, is that upon the Supertonic, and the following Exercises show
the employment of this chord, correctly prepared and resolved, in its
root position and inversions :—

Ex. 146.

Ex. 147 shows a progression of Diatonic chords of the seventh,
employed sequentially. Except in such progressions, a chord of the
seventh upon the Subdominant resolving upon a chord of the seventh
upon the Leading-note triad, as at (*a*), is rarely employed. The
sequential nature of the progression also explains the doubled Leading-
note, at (*a*). It will be noticed that in every other chord of the seventh,
the fifth is omitted. This is necessary to avoid a progression of
consecutive fifths :—

Ex. 147.

153. The figuring of diatonic chords of the seventh and their
inversions is the same as the figuring of the chord of the Dominant
seventh and its inversions, both being made up of a note with its third,
fifth, and seventh. The difference between the various chords of the
seventh is determined solely by the *quality* of the several intervals, and
of this the figuring takes no account, unless it is necessary to express it
by means of accidentals.

EXERCISES.

I.—Construct progressions similar to those in Ex. 146, showing the
employment of a diatonic chord of the seventh upon the Supertonic,
and all its inversions, correctly prepared and resolved, in the keys of
A major and F minor.

Harmonize the following, introducing a diatonic chord of the seventh
at each of the places indicated. The root position to be employed in
(II), the first inversion in (III), the second inversion in (IV), and the

last inversion in (V). Note carefully the places where modulations occur :—

Harmonize the following, in accordance with the figuring :—

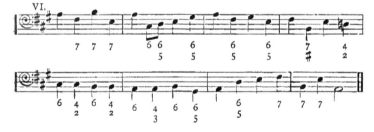

CHAPTER XXII.

UNESSENTIAL NOTES.—AUXILIARY NOTES, PASSING NOTES, AND
ANTICIPATIONS.

[There are no separate **Ear Exercises** *given in connection with this chapter, but most of the musical examples will be found suitable for employment as such, having been constructed with this end in view.]*

154. Notes which are sounded in connection with chords of which they do not form a real or essential part, are called UNESSENTIAL NOTES. Thus, in the following example, in which the common chord of C is repeated throughout three bars, the notes, (indicated by asterisks), which do not form part of this chord, but which are employed in connection with the several notes of the chord to elaborate the treble part in the first bar, and the bass part in the second bar, are *Unessential Notes.*

Ex. 148.

As unessential notes are always dissonant against the prevailing harmony, they are also frequently described as UNESSENTIAL DISCORDS. Two of the most important, as well as the most useful kinds of unessential notes, are AUXILIARY NOTES and PASSING NOTES, both of which will be considered in the present chapter, while another kind, almost equally important, called SUSPENSIONS, will be considered in the next chapter.

155. **AUXILIARY NOTES.**—Auxiliary notes are unessential notes formed at the distance of a second, either above or below the harmony notes *to which they proceed,* and which form their *Resolution.* An auxiliary note may be approached either by step, as in Ex. 149 (*a*), or by leap, as in (*b*); or it may be preceded by a rest, as in (*c*). When an auxiliary note is approached by step, as in (*a*), it is always preceded and followed by the same harmony note.

Ex. 119.

An auxiliary note may be formed either between harmony notes belonging to the same chord, as in Ex. 149, or between harmony notes belonging to different chords, as in Ex. 150.

Ex. 150.

156. The formation of auxiliary notes is subject to the following conditions :—

I.—An auxiliary note formed *above* the harmony note upon which it resolves, *whether approached by step or by leap*, should be the next degree above in the diatonic scale, thus :—

Ex. 151.

II.—An auxiliary note formed *below* the harmony note upon which it resolves, *when approached by step*, should, if the harmony note be either the root, or the fifth of the chord, be a semitone below, as at (*a*) and (*b*) respectively ; but if the harmony note be the third of the chord, the auxiliary note may be at the distance of either a semitone or a tone, as at (*c*) and (*d*) respectively :—

Ex. 152.

III.—An auxiliary note formed *below* the harmony note upon
which it resolves, *when approached by leap*, is almost invariably at the
distance of a semitone below, see Ex. 153. An auxiliary note so
formed, may be approached by the leap of an Augmented interval, if
desired.

Ex. 153.

IV.—An auxiliary note which is formed a semitone below a harmony
note, is almost invariably written as a Diatonic semitone below, as in
Ex. 153, and *not* as a Chromatic semitone below, as in Ex. 154.

Ex. 154.

157. **PASSING NOTES.**—A Passing note is an unessential
note approached by step from a harmony note, but which, instead of
returning to the same harmony note (as in the case of an Auxiliary note
approached by step) continues or "passes" on in the same direction, and
resolves upon another harmony note, as in Ex. 155. The harmony
notes upon either side of a Passing note may be harmonized by the
same chord, as in (*a*), or by different chords, as in (*b*).

Ex. 155.

A Passing note, instead of being followed immediately by a harmony
note, may be followed by another Passing note, provided the melody
thus formed still proceeds in the *same* direction until a harmony
note is reached, as in Ex. 156 (*a*). It is incorrect to change the
direction of the movement immediately after the second passing note,
as in (*b*).

Ex. 156.

158. Chromatic Passing Notes.—Chromatic passing notes as well as Diatonic ones may be employed if desired, but when a Chromatic passing note is introduced in a series of passing notes, the passage must then continue according to the Chromatic scale, that is, *by semitones*, until a harmony note is reached, as in (*a*), and not as in (*b*).

Ex. 157.

159. The employment of the Melodic Minor Scale.—In the Minor key, both the Major sixth and the Minor seventh of the Melodic Minor Scale, may be employed as Auxiliary notes or as Passing notes, in either ascending or descending passages, thus :—

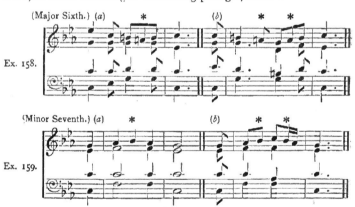

Ex. 158.

Ex. 159.

160. Accented Auxiliary Notes and Passing Notes.—Although Auxiliary notes and Passing notes are generally employed upon the weaker beats of a bar, or upon the weaker portions of individual beats, yet they may also be employed upon the strong beats, or upon the stronger portion of individual beats. In such positions they are similar in nature to appoggiaturas, thus :—

Ex. 160.

161. **False Relation and Unessential Notes.**—In the above example, there is no incorrect False Relation created between the F sharp in the Treble part and the F natural in the Alto and Bass parts of the previous chord. The following rule refers to this and all similar passages. *Chromatic unessential notes, when correctly formed and resolved, do not create incorrect False Relation with the harmony notes of their own chord or of adjacent chords* (see also Ex. 157).

162. **Changing Notes.**—Either an Auxiliary note or a Passing note may, instead of immediately resolving upon a harmony note, leap a third to another unessential note beyond this harmony note, the second unessential note then proceeding to the harmony note, which would have been the resolution of the first unessential note. The elaboration of (*a*) to form (*b*) illustrates these points :—

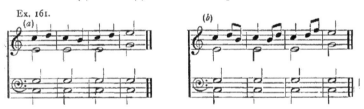

Ex. 161.

The two unessential notes so formed next to one another, are called CHANGING NOTES.

Auxiliary notes, having some resemblance to " changing notes," may be formed by the elaboration of a series of two or more adjacent harmony notes, the auxiliary notes leaping a third to their resolution, thus :—

Ex. 162.

163. **Unessential Notes in two parts.**—Unessential notes may move together in two parts, or one part may be formed of unessential notes and the other of harmony notes, while some of the essential notes of the chord are sustained, as shown in Ex. 163, where the unessential notes are indicated by asterisks. In such cases the progression formed by the joint movement of these two parts must be correct, quite apart from their relation to the notes of the chord which are remaining stationary, thus:—

Ex. 163.

Bad.

Passing notes proceeding in two parts by contrary motion, may continue on in the same direction, irrespective of the dissonances which are created by their progression, until they simultaneously reach harmony notes, thus:—

Ex. 164.

When auxiliary notes proceed in two parts in thirds or sixths, they may be situated at the distance of either a tone or a semitone from their resolution, provided both parts move diatonically, as in Ex. 165 (*a*), but if either part move a semitone which is produced by chromatic alteration, the other part *must* also move a semitone as at (*b*) and (*c*):—

Ex. 165.

164. **Anticipations.**—When one or more notes of a chord are proceeded to previously to the other notes of the same chord, such notes are said to be *anticipated*, and the note or notes which form the anticipation, and which are always upon a weaker beat, or a weaker part of a beat, than the note or notes which they anticipate, are called ANTICIPATIONS, thus:—

Ex. 166.

165. HARMONIC PROGRESSION in connection with Unessential Notes.—Most of the rules of progression which have already been given in connection with harmony notes, apply also to progressions into the formation of which Auxiliary notes or Passing notes enter.* All such faulty progressions as those illustrated below, although entirely due to the introduction of Auxiliary notes, are forbidden :—

Ex. 167.

Although, as shown above, the introduction of unessential notes may easily change a correct progression into an incorrect one, yet their introduction will never change an incorrect progression into a correct one. Thus, the forbidden consecutives between the harmony notes in the following are bad, in spite of the passing notes which come between them :—

Ex. 168.

166. The following rules of progression must be borne in mind when working the Exercises at the end of this chapter. *No two parts may proceed by oblique motion from a second to a unison,* as in Ex. 169 (*a*), but the reverse of this progression, to proceed from a unison to a second, as in (*b*), is perfectly good :—

* This statement, from the *composer's* point of view, is not strictly accurate, but as far as the *student of Harmony* is concerned, in matters of progression, no "exceptional progressions," such as those mentioned in the chapter upon Exceptional Progression (Part II), should be allowed in these early stages.

Ex. 169.

Bad.　　　Good.

This rule applies both to essential (or harmony notes) and unessential notes (see par. 129).

No two parts may proceed in seconds, (or ninths), or sevenths, with one another. Such progressions as the following, in which consecutive seconds and sevenths are formed by the employment of unessential notes proceeding to notes belonging to inversions of the Dominant Seventh, should be avoided :—

Ex. 170.

167. Consecutive Perfect fourths with the Bass.—*Consecutive Perfect fourths with the bass* (though forbidden when both fourths form part of second inversions of common chords), *are allowed when the second fourth is an unessential note*, as the F in the following example :—

Ex. 171.

Good.

EXERCISES.

I.—Taking Ex. 149 (*a*) and (*b*) as your models, show the formation of *Auxiliary Notes*, both above and below *each* of the notes of the Tonic triad, in the keys of E flat major and F sharp minor, the auxiliary notes to be approached (1) by step, and (2) by leap, from a note of the same chord.

II.—Show the formation of *Auxiliary Notes* between notes of the Tonic and Submediant triads, and between notes of the Tonic and Dominant triads, or their inversions, in the keys of A major and G minor, the auxiliary notes to be approached (1) by step, and (2) by leap. (Models, Ex. 150 (*a*) and (*b*)).

I

III.—Show the formation of *Passing Notes*, both ascending and descending, between each of the notes of the Tonic triad in the keys of D major and F minor (see Ex. 155 (*a*)).

IV.—Show the formation of *Passing Notes*, both ascending and descending, between notes of the Tonic and Subdominant triads, and between notes of the Tonic and Submediant Triads, in the keys of B flat major and E minor (see Ex. 155 (*b*)).

V.—Show the formation of *Changing Notes* in connection with each of the notes of the Tonic triad, in the keys of D flat major and B minor (see Ex. 161).

VI—Show the formation of *Anticipations* in the treble part, in connection with Perfect cadences in the keys of E major and D minor.

VII.—Show the formation of unessential notes in *two parts*, in connection with the Tonic triad in the keys of G major and B minor (see Ex. 163).

Harmonize the following, treating the notes indicated, as unessential notes :—

Harmonize the following in accordance with the figuring. Any figuring which may seem unfamiliar to the pupil, will, when the passage is filled up, be found due to the employment of Passing notes:—

CHAPTER XXIII.

SUSPENSIONS.

168. A SUSPENSION is a note tied or suspended over a chord of which it forms no essential part, but to one of the notes of which it can pass by moving the step of a second. Thus, in Ex. 172, the notes in the treble part, which are sustained from the previous chord over the chord of C (indicated by asterisks), and then proceed to a note of that chord by moving the step of a second, are called SUSPENSIONS.

Ex. 172.

169. A suspension must be present as an essential or harmony note in the immediately preceding chord to that in which it is suspended, and it must be heard *in the same part as that in which it appears as a suspension*. The harmony note in the preceding chord which is identical with it, and to which it is generally tied, is called THE NOTE OF PREPARATION or simply THE PREPARATION, and this note should be at least equal in length to the suspension itself. The note to which the suspension proceeds, is called THE NOTE OF RESOLUTION or simply THE RESOLUTION. A suspension always occurs either upon a stronger beat, or upon the stronger portion of a beat, than the note upon which it resolves. The most useful suspensions are, the suspension of the note above the root of a triad, shown in Ex. 172 (*a*), called the 9 8 SUSPENSION, and the suspension of the note above the third of a triad, shown in (*b*), and called the 4 3 SUSPENSION. The suspension of the note above the fifth of a triad, shown in (*c*), and called the 6 5 SUSPENSION, is less useful than either of the others, and its character as a suspension is somewhat ambiguous. It is more frequently met with in an inverted form than in its root position.

170. **Retardations.**—It is possible for some suspensions to resolve by rising a second instead of falling one, they are then frequently called RETARDATIONS. The most important of these is the suspended or retarded Leading-note. This is generally suspended over the Tonic

triad, as in Ex. 173 (*a*), when it becomes a 7 8 SUSPENSION OR RETARDA-
TION. It may also be employed over the Submediant (see par. 186).
The suspended ninth is occasionally resolved by rising to the tenth, (or
third), as in (*b*), but this form of resolution is rare.

Ex. 173.

THE 9 8 SUSPENSION.

171. As was stated above, a note which is suspended over a triad,
and is resolved by falling a second to the root of that triad, is called a
9 8 SUSPENSION. This suspension is figured simply 9 8, the 9 implying
the other notes of the chord.

Ex. 174.

Provided this suspension is correctly prepared and resolved, it may
be employed in its root position in connection with any triad in either
major or minor key, with the exception of the triad upon the
Leading-note, with which it can never be employed, as its resolution
would involve the doubling of this note. Its employment in connection
with the dissonant triads upon the Supertonic and Mediant of the
minor key is, however, rare.

Ear Exercises, (also in C minor, except the fourth exercise) :—

Ex. 175.

172. In this suspension the suspended note, which may appear in either of the upper parts, must always be not less than a ninth above the root of the chord, whether the root be present only in the bass or doubled in one of the inner parts. That is to say, the ninth may *never* be employed at the interval of a second from the root when this is sounded simultaneously with the ninth, as in the following example (see par. 166) :—

Ex. 176.

Bad.   Bad.

173. **Ornamental Resolutions.**—A suspension, before proceeding to its regular resolution, may first of all move to some other note of the chord, from which it may proceed either direct to its regular resolution, as in Ex. 177 (*a*), or by means of one or more intermediate notes, as in (*b*) and (*c*). In these cases, what are called "ornamental resolutions" of the suspension are formed. Another, and even more familiar form of ornamental resolution, is shown in (*d*).

Ear Exercises (also in C minor) :—

Ex. 177.

174. **Exceptional Resolutions.**—In the resolution of suspensions, it is possible at the resolution *to change the position of the chord* of which the suspension forms part, as in Ex. 178 (*a*), where the suspension is over a triad in its root position, while the resolution takes place upon the first inversion of this triad. A more exceptional form of resolution

is for a *change of chord* to take place at the resolution, as in (*b*), where the suspended note appears as a ninth above C, but is resolved upon the third of the triad of A. In such resolutions the figuring must be modified according.

Ex. 178.

175. **The Doubling of Notes.**—In a suspension, the notes of the chord which may be doubled are the same as if the suspension were not present, such doubling however is subject to the following special condition :— *When the note upon which a suspension resolves is sounded in one of the upper parts simultaneously with the suspension itself, (not of course at the same pitch, but at the distance of one or more octaves), it must be approached by step in the contrary direction to which the suspension resolves,* thus :—

Ex. 179.

Good.   Not good.

176. **Harmonic Progression.**—As a suspension is an unessential note which only temporarily takes the place of a harmony note, *progressions which are incorrect without a suspension cannot be corrected by the introduction of a suspension,* thus :—

Ex. 180.

Bad.   Bad.

Paragraphs 173 to 176 refer to ALL suspensions and inversions of such.

EXERCISES.

Taking the Ear Exercises, Ex. 175, as your models, construct a series of progressions showing the 9 8 suspension *correctly prepared and resolved*, and employed in connection with all the available common chords and triads in the keys of E major and F minor.

*** The Augmented second between the sixth and seventh degrees of the Harmonic Minor Scale, prevents the suspension of the Leading-note in the Minor key, in suspensions which resolve *downward*. This should be borne in mind when working the above, and all Exercises of a similar nature.

Harmonize the following, introducing a 9 8 suspension, correctly prepared and resolved, at each of the places indicated :—

Taking the Ear Exercises, Ex. 177, as your models, construct a series of progressions, showing different ornamental resolutions of the 9 8 suspension in connection with (*a*) the Tonic Triad, and (*b*) the Subdominant Triad, in the keys of E major and G minor.

177. **First Inversion :—**

Ex. 181.

The third of the original chord now being in the bass, the suspended ninth has become a suspended seventh resolving upon the sixth, both being accompanied by the third from the bass, that is, the fifth of the original chord. The figuring of this Suspension, which is simply 7 6, must not be confused with the figuring of the chords of the seventh, in which the figure 7 includes a 5 as well as a 3. In the filling up of figured basses, an examination of the chord upon which the 7 resolves, will show conclusively whether the chord indicated by the 7 is an essential discord or a suspension.

Ear Exercises :—

Ex. 182.

(Also in C minor.)   (Also in C minor.)

As a chord of the sixth may be employed upon every degree of both major and minor scales, this suspension may also be employed upon every degree upon which it can be correctly prepared and resolved.

EXERCISES.

Construct a series of progressions showing the first inversion of the 9 8 suspension (7 6) correctly prepared and resolved, and employed in connection with all the available chords of the sixth in the keys of A flat major and F sharp minor. (Models, Ex 182.)

Harmonize the following, introducing the first inversion of the 9 8 suspension at each of the places indicated :—

178. **Second Inversion:**—

Ex. 183.

The fifth of the original chord now being in the bass, the suspended ninth has become a suspended fifth resolving upon the fourth, both being accompanied by the sixth from the bass, that is, the third of the original chord. The figuring of this chord must not be confused with the figuring of the first inversion of chords of the seventh. The nature of the resolution will conclusively determine which chord is intended, when such chords are indicated only by figures over a bass note.

Ear Exercises (also in C minor) :—

Ex. 184.

The progression of the bass part of this inversion is of course subject to the same restrictions as those which govern the progression of the bass part of $\frac{6}{4}$ chords generally (see par 96).

EXERCISES.

Construct a series of progressions showing the second inversion of the 9 8 suspension $\left(\begin{smallmatrix}6 & - \\ 5 & 4\end{smallmatrix}\right)$ correctly prepared and resolved, and employed in connection with each of the Primary triads in the keys of B major and G minor. (Models, Ex. 184.)

Harmonize the following, introducing the second inversion of the 9 8 suspension at each of the places indicated :—

179. The Inversion with the Suspension in the Bass :—

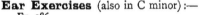

The suspended ninth of the original chord being now in the lowest part, the other notes of the chord are a second, a fourth, and a seventh above the suspended note, and become, respectively, a third, a fifth and an octave from the note upon which the suspension resolves. When the root is heard simultaneously with the suspension, as in the above example, it must be approached by step in the opposite direction to the resolution of the suspension (see par. 175). When the root is not present the figuring of the chord is simply $\begin{smallmatrix}4 & - \\ 2 & -\end{smallmatrix}$. This $\begin{smallmatrix}4 & - \\ 2 & -\end{smallmatrix}$ must not be confused with the same figures when representing the last inversion of a chord of the seventh.

Ear Exercises (also in C minor) :—

Ex. 186.

(see par. 71.)

In this inversion, progressions like the following, which are incorrect without the suspension, must be carefully avoided (see par. 176):—

Ex. 187.

Bad.

EXERCISES.

Construct a series of progressions, showing the 9 8 suspension correctly prepared and resolved and employed in the bass, in connection with all the available common chords in the keys of E flat major and B minor. (Models, Ex. 186.)

Harmonize the following, introducing the last inversion of the 9 8 suspension at each of the places indicated:—

Harmonize the following in accordance with the figures:—

THE 4 3 SUSPENSION.

180. When a note which is suspended over a chord is resolved by falling a second to the third of that chord, it is called a 4 3 SUSPENSION OR A SUSPENDED FOURTH:—

Ex. 188.

In its root position, this suspension being generally accompanied by the perfect fifth from the bass, is rarely employed except over those degrees of the scale upon which common chords can be formed, and the figures 4 3 imply the fifth, which is always present with the fourth. When employed over the Dominant it is frequently accompanied by the chord of the Dominant seventh. The figuring is then $\begin{smallmatrix} 7 & - \\ 4 & 3 \end{smallmatrix}$.

Ear Exercises (also in C minor):—

Ex. 189.
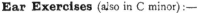

In this suspension either the root or the fifth should be doubled. The third, when a minor third, however, and when approached by step, as in the third exercise above, is sometimes heard simultaneously with the suspended fourth at the distance of a ninth, but never at the distance of a second.

EXERCISES.

Taking the above Ear Exercises as your models, construct a series of progressions showing the 4 3 suspension, correctly prepared and resolved, and employed in connection with all the available common chords in the keys of E flat major and G sharp minor.

Harmonize the following, introducing a 4 3 suspension, correctly prepared and resolved, at each of the places indicated:—

Construct a series of progressions, showing different ornamental resolutions of the 4 3 suspension in connection with (*a*) the Tonic Triad, and (*b*) the Dominant Triad, in the keys of A flat major and F sharp minor (see Ex. 177).

181. **First Inversion**:—

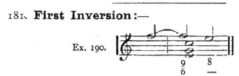

Ex. 190.

The third being in the bass, the suspended fourth has now become a suspended ninth resolving upon the octave, both being accompanied by the third and sixth from the bass. This inversion cannot be employed upon the Leading-note as it would involve the doubling of this note.

Ear Exercises (also in C minor):—

Ex. 191.

EXERCISES.

Construct a series of progressions, showing the first inversion of the 4 3 suspension ($\frac{9}{6}$ $\frac{8}{6}$) correctly prepared and resolved, in connection with all the available first inversions of triads, in the keys of A flat major and C sharp minor. (Models, Ex. 191.)

Harmonize the following, introducing the first inversion of the 4 3 suspension at each of the places indicated :—

182. **Second Inversion**:—

Ex. 192.

The fifth of the original chord being in the bass, the suspended fourth has now become a suspended seventh resolving upon the sixth, both being accompanied by the fourth from the bass, which is the root of the chord. The progression of the bass note of this inversion, is of course subject to the same rules as those which govern the progression of the bass notes of $\frac{6}{4}$ chords generally. (See par. 96.)

Ear Exercises (also in C minor):—

Ex. 193.

EXERCISES.

Construct a series of progressions showing the second inversion of the 4 3 suspension $\left(\begin{smallmatrix}7 & 6\\4 & -\end{smallmatrix}\right)$, correctly prepared and resolved, in connection with the second inversion of each of the Primary triads, in the keys of A major and E flat minor. (Models, Ex. 193.)

Harmonize the following, introducing the second inversion of the 4 3 suspension at each of the places indicated :—

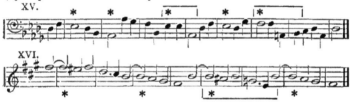

---

183. **The Inversion with the Suspension in the Bass:**—

Ex. 194.

The suspension now being in the lowest part, the root and fifth of the original chord are a fifth and a second above the suspended note, and become a sixth and a third when this falls to its resolution.

Ear Exercises (also in C minor) :—

Ex. 195.

EXERCISES.

Construct a series of progressions showing the 4 3 suspension employed in the bass $\left(\begin{smallmatrix}5 & —\\ 2 & —\end{smallmatrix}\right)$, correctly prepared and resolved, in connection with all the available first inversions of triads in the keys of E major and B flat minor. (Models, Ex. 195.)

Harmonize the following, introducing the 4 3 suspension with the suspension in the bass at each of the places indicated :—

(see par. 71).

Harmonize the following in accordance with the figures :—

THE 6 5 SUSPENSION.

184. When a note which is suspended over a chord, is resolved by falling a second to the fifth of that chord, it is called a 6 5 SUSPENSION.

Ex. 196.

6   5

It is quite possible to explain this suspension as made up of two different chords, namely, as the first inversion of a triad, followed by a triad upon the same bass note. Only when the suspension and its resolution are sounded simultaneously, is the character of the chord as a suspension clearly defined. In this form, it is perhaps most useful in its second inversion, as shown in Ex. 197 (*c*), although it is not a very familiar chord in any form, or in any inversion. The figuring of the different inversions is given below.

Ear Exercises (also in C minor):—

EXERCISES.

Taking the above Ear Exercises as your models, construct similar series of progressions showing the 6 5 suspension, and its inversions, correctly prepared and resolved, in connection with the Tonic triad, in the keys of B flat major and E minor.

Harmonize the following, introducing the 6 5 suspension, or one of its inversions, at each of the places indicated. The letters refer to the different positions of the chord as illustrated in the Ear Exercises :—

Harmonize the following in accordance with the figures :—

THE SUSPENDED (OR RETARDED) LEADING-NOTE.

185. All the suspensions which fall a second to their resolution have now been considered, and there only remains one other suspension to be referred to, that is, THE SUSPENDED (OR RETARDED) LEADING-NOTE, when it resolves by *rising* a second to the Tonic. When the Leading-note is suspended in this manner over the Tonic chord, it forms a 7 8 suspension, the 7 in this suspension including both a 5 and a 3, thus:—

Ex. 198.

This suspension may be employed in any of its inversions, but like the 6 5 suspension, its character as a suspension is only clearly defined when the suspended note and its resolution are sounded simultaneously, as in the first and last examples given below. The figuring of the suspension in the different positions in which it is generally employed, is shown below.

Ear Exercises (also in C minor):—

Ex. 199.

186. The Leading-note may be suspended and resolved in a similar manner over the Submediant, either in connection with a triad upon this note, as shown in Ex. 200 (*a*), or in connection with the first inversion of the Subdominant triad, as shown in (*b*), but in these forms it more frequently occurs in double and triple suspensions (see par. 187-8) than as a single suspension.

Ear Exercises (also in C minor):—

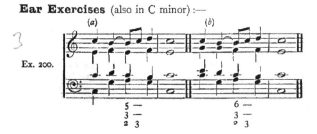

Ex. 200.

K

EXERCISES.

Taking the Ear Exercises, Exs. 199 and 200, as your models, construct similar series of progressions showing the employment of the suspended Leading-note in connection with (1) the Tonic chord in its root position and inversions, (2) the Submediant triad, and (3) the first inversion of the Subdominant triad, in the keys of F sharp major and G minor.

Harmonize the following, introducing the suspended Leading-note in connection with the Tonic triad, or an inversion of it, at each of the places indicated :—

Harmonize the following in accordance with the figuring :—

DOUBLE SUSPENSIONS.

187. When two notes are suspended simultaneously over the same chord, upon the essential notes of which they resolve by each note moving the step of a second, they form what is called a DOUBLE SUSPENSION. The most useful forms of double suspensions are combinations of 9 8 and 4 3, 9 8 and 7 8, and 7 8 and 4 3. Ex. 201 illustrates some of the most familiar forms of these :—

Ear Exercises (also in C minor) :—

Ex. 201.

EXERCISES.

Taking the above Ear Exercises as your models construct similar series of progressions showing the employment of the various forms of double suspensions, correctly prepared and resolved, in connection with the Tonic triad in the keys of G major and F minor.

Harmonize the following, introducing a double suspension at each of the places indicated :—

Harmonize the following in accordance with the figures :—

XXX.

TRIPLE SUSPENSIONS
and the Suspension of Complete Chords.

188. When three notes are suspended over a bass note, the chord so formed is called either a TRIPLE SUSPENSION OR THE SUSPENSION OF A COMPLETE CHORD. The most familiar combination of this kind is the suspension of the chord of the Dominant Seventh over either the Tonic or the Submediant, as shown below, Ex. 202 (*a*) and (*b*), but any chord may be suspended over a bass note to which it does not belong, provided the several notes of the suspended chord can each move by step to the notes of the triad belonging to this bass note, without forming incorrect progressions.

Ear Exercises :—

Ex. 202.

(also in C minor.)

189. **The figuring of Suspensions.**—There is perhaps no class of chords, the figuring of which will give the pupil so much trouble, or is likely to bewilder him to such an extent, as suspensions, or we might say the inversions of suspensions. Especially will this be the case if he attempts to analyse these simply by reference to their figures. Such a course can only lead, ultimately, to mental confusion, both with regard to the suspensions themselves, and also with regard to the other chords, whose figuring more or less resembles that of some of the suspensions. The only safe method in such matters is (1) to examine the nature of the chord itself in notes (not in figures), and (2) to examine the nature of its resolution.

190. **Suspensions in connection with Discords.**—Suspensions are generally employed in connection with triads and their inversions, but, provided they are correctly prepared and resolved, they may be also employed in connection with discords, the only suspension however, which is at all frequently employed in connection with such, is the 4 3 suspension. This suspension has already been shown in connection with the chord of the Dominant seventh.

EXERCISES.

Taking Ex. 202 (*a*) and (*b*) as your models, construct similar progressions showing the employment of triple suspensions in connection with the Tonic and Submediant triads, in the keys of E major and B flat minor.

Harmonize the following, introducing a triple suspension at each of the places indicated :—

Harmonize the following in accordance with the figures :—

INDEX.

[The numbers always refer to the Paragraphs except in those instances in which it is otherwise stated].

END OF PART I.

MUSICAL MEMORY

AND ITS CULTIVATION,

ALSO AN

INVESTIGATION INTO THE FORMS OF MEMORY EMPLOYED IN PIANO-
FORTE PLAYING, AND A THEORY AS TO THE RELATIVE
EXTENT OF THE EMPLOYMENT OF SUCH FORMS.

A GUIDE TO THE MEMORIZING OF PIANOFORTE MUSIC.

Price Two Shillings and Sixpence.

"*THE TIMES*" *says :—*

"Of books on the technique of music, none lately published has been executed with more skill and certainty than 'Musical Memory,' a small treatise that will be of the utmost service to the many who must find what is called the 'memorizing' of music a formidable task. The soundness of the methods recommended, and the practical experience which appears on every page, call for nothing but praise."

"*THE DAILY GRAPHIC*" *says :—*

"An interesting little book on musical memory. It is clearly written, and many of the hints and suggestions with regard to memorizations will be valuable to students."

"*THE SUNDAY TIMES*" *says :—*

"I commend to the perusal of musicians generally—young and old, professional and amateur—Dr. Shinn's clever little book. Fascinating as the subject is, it has never before been treated by a writer from a scientific standpoint or reduced to a system upon lines definite enough to be followed and utilized by either teacher or student."

"*THE OBSERVER*" *says :—*

"He has treated his subject in a thoroughly scientific and therefore practical manner, and has at the same time so worded his remarks that the least scientifically-minded reader may understand them."

"*THE GUARDIAN*" *says :—*

"Dr. Shinn has evidently made a deep study of the subject, and his little essay is extremely able and interesting."

"*THE MUSICAL TIMES*" *says :—*

"Dr. Shinn not merely theorizes on a subject about which no literature seems to exist, but by copious musical examples gives practical proof of the truth that is in him. —We unhesitatingly commend this excellent treatise."

"*THE MUSICAL NEWS*" *says :—*

"The author has laid the musical world under a debt by the publication of a capital little book upon a subject far too long left unstudied. His book will amply repay the most careful and thoughtful perusal."

"*THE I.S.M. JOURNAL*" *says :—*

"An able and extensive treatise, and one which has evidently been the outcome of much experimental research."

"*THE MUSICAL HERALD*" *says :—*

"An excellent work, in which the subject is treated by its author in a truly philosophic spirit. —We heartily recommend it to all pianoforte teachers."

THE VINCENT MUSIC CO., Ltd., 60, BERNERS ST., LONDON, W.

BY THE SAME AUTHOR.

Elementary Ear-Training,

BOOK I.—MELODIC.

A Method of Training the Ear to Perceive and to Discriminate Relations of Pitch, Relations of Strength, and Relations of Length, in so far as these constitute the Elements of Musical Sounds, and on the Writing of the same from Dictation;

WITH

Over 750 Graduated Ear-Tests and Dictation Exercises.

Price Two Shillings.

The Times says :—" A thoughtful little treatise."

The Sunday Times says :—" A valuable addition to the select store of musical text books published by Mr. Vincent. Teachers of the young especially, will appreciate the practical form in which the author has here embodied his hints for training the untutored mind to grasp the various relations of pitch, strength and length."

The Musical News says :—" A crystallisation into convenient form, of the many appeals which have been recently made on behalf of a broader and deeper consideration of this vital part of the music teacher's duty, and a handy guide in the discharge of that duty. . . . suitable for immediate introduction into classes as a text book."

The Musical Courier says :—" As a contribution to the systematic training of that organ upon which music makes special demands, Dr. Shinn's book deserves high commendation, the subject being treated in a practical manner, and presented in a form useful to the teacher and easily comprehensible to the learner."

The I.S.M. Journal says :—" It presents a thoroughly practical and well considered system, and one, moreover, which can only be the result of considerable practical experience. We recommend it very heartily to all teachers of music."

THE VINCENT MUSIC CO., Ltd., 60, BERNERS STREET, LONDON, **W.**

Theoretical Works and Music Text Books.

		Net.
		s. d.
Elementary Ear-Training	Fred G Shinn	2 0
Rudiments of Musical Knowledge	C W Pearce	1 0
Rudiments of Music for Choirs and Schools	Harvey Lohr	0 6
Manual of Sight Singing, Part I. Paper Cover, 1s., Cloth, 1s 6d	F. J. Sawyer	
" " Part II. Paper Cover, 1s., Cloth, 1s 6d	" "	
Graded School Song-Book.		
Designed for use with The Manual of Sight Singing, ten parts, each 2d Complete in Paper Cover, 1s 4d , in Cloth, 2s	" "	
Choral Instructor for Treble Voices	C Vincent	0 8
New-Century Pianoforte Method	"	2 0
School of Arpeggio Fingering (Practical)	S Myerscough	3 0
Harmony, Diatonic and Chromatic	C. Vincent	3 0
Tonality and Roots	A J Greenish	1 6
Students' Counterpoint	C W Pearce	2 0
Composers' Counterpoint	" "	2 0
Form in Music	J. Humfrey Anger	3 0
Scoring for an Orchestra	C. Vincent	1 6
The Reading of Music	M. E P Zeper	1 6
Combined Rhythms	R I. Rowe	0 8
Musical Memory and its Cultivation	Fred G Shinn	2 6
On Organ Playing	A. Page	2 0
Voice Culture	Guido Porpora	3 0
Hints to Singers	R. T. White	0 3
300 Examination Questions	A. Mangelsdorff	1 6
Score Reading in the various Clefs, 48 Fugues, 2 Vols	J. S Bach each	4 0
How we Hear (A Treatise on Sound)	F C. Baker	1 6
Vocal Exercises for Choir Boys	F. N. Baxter	0 1
Practical Suggestions for Training Choir Boys	E G Bentall	0 6
Voice Exercises for Boys	"	0 2
On Mendelssohn's Organ Sonatas	C. W. Pearce	2 0
Scales and Arpeggios	S. Midgley	3 0
The Art of Violin Bowing	Paul Stoeving	3 0
Choir Training based on Voice Production	A. Madeley Richardson	2 6
The Psalms, their Structure and Musical Rendering	"	3 0
Training of Men's Voices	R I. White	0 6
Memorizing Major and Minor Scales	F A. Clarke	0 3
Rudiments of Vocal Music	T. L Southgate	0 2
Vocal Exercises on the Old Italian System	E G White	2 6
The Brass Band and how to Write for It	C Vincent	2 6
A History of Music	E Duncan	2 6
Studies in Musical Graces	E Fowles	3 0
Key to Ditto		1 6
Melodies and How to Harmonize Them	E Duncan	3 0
Key to Ditto	"	2 0
What Music is	Duncan Hume	1 6
Plain-Song and Gregorian Music	F. Burgess	2 6
Words in Singing	C J. Brennan	1 6
Organ Accompaniment to the Psalms	C. W Pearce	2 0
Dictionary of Organ Stops	J. I Wedgwood	5 0
A Treatise on Harmony, Part I & Part II	J. Humfrey Anger each	3 0
Voice Training Exercises and Studies	F. C. Field Hyde	4 0
The First Principles of Voice Production	Thomas Kelly	0 6
Practical Points for Choral Singers	Robert Simmons	1 0
The Organist's Directory	C W. Pearce	3 0
The Indispensible Theory Book	Woodrow & Rudd	1 0
Graded Score Reading (C and G Clefs)	F J Sawyer	2 6
Primer of Part-Singing, Two Books	F. J Sawyer each	1 0
A Method of Teaching Harmony	Fred G Shinn	
Part I—Diatonic Harmony. Cloth boards, 3s., Limp covers, 2s 6d		
" II—Chromatic Harmony. " " 3s , " " 2s 6d.		

The VINCENT MUSIC CO. Ltd., 60, Berners St., London, W.

Milton Keynes UK
Ingram Content Group UK Ltd.
UKHW021029231024
2330UKWH00037B/217